Scrambles & Easy Climbs in the Lake District

First published in 2003 by Grey Stone Books

British Library Cataloguing in Publication Data

A catalogue record of this book is available from the British Library.

ISBN 978-0-9515996-9-3

Conventional mapping has been based on copyright material from Harvey Maps, Main Street Doune, Perthshire, Scotland and a licence has been issued

While every effort has been taken by the authors to ensure the accuracy of this book, changes do occur, and these may affect the contents. Neither the author nor the publisher accepts liability for these.

It is expected that walkers and climbers, or their companions, will be fully experienced in mountaincraft before setting out on the more serious expeditions.

Printed by Carnmor Print and Design, London Road, Preston

Scrambles & Easy Climbs in the Lake District

Jon Sparks & Judith Brown

Editor; Ronald Turnbull
Maps, sketches and line drawings by John Gillham
with licence from Harvey Maps

Grey Stone Books, Hoddlesden

Acknowledgments
The Scottish Mountaineering Club's excellent 'Skye Scrambles', compiled by Noel Williams, showed us the value of a guide which bridges the arbitrary division between scrambles and climbs. Brian Evans has done a fantastic job documenting the scrambles in the Lake District, while the Fell and Rock Climbing Club has done the same for its rock-climbing.

Jon Sparks
I must thank everyone with whom I have climbed and scrambled in the Lakes, but above all my partner, Bernie Carter, whose summer has been ruled, yet again, by a book. For unstinting support, for encouragement when I didn't feel like going out, for sharing so many climbs and scrambles, and for almost never complaining, my gratitude is boundless.

Judith Brown
I want to give a big thank you to all the members of Keswick Mountaineering Club who tied onto me to research these routes. Some are old hands, for others it was their first visit to the big crags of Scafell and Pillar. I only hope that the experience has inspired them to go back, and not put them off for life. Finally, a big thank you to Jon for involving me in this project and to Bernie who suggested it.

Photos: All photos, unless stated are by Jon Sparks Photography

Front Cover: Judith Brown on the first pitch of Main Wall, Gimmer Crag (Gt Langdale)
Rear Cover: Top: scrambling up Whiteside Gill on Helvellyn; middle: On Little Blake Rigg, Duddon Valley; bottom: Jon Sparks on the 1st pitch of Trinity Slabs

Updates

As with all Grey Stone Books we intend to keep Scrambles and Easy Climbs in the Lake District up to date. Visit our website for information

www.grey-stone.co.uk

Contents

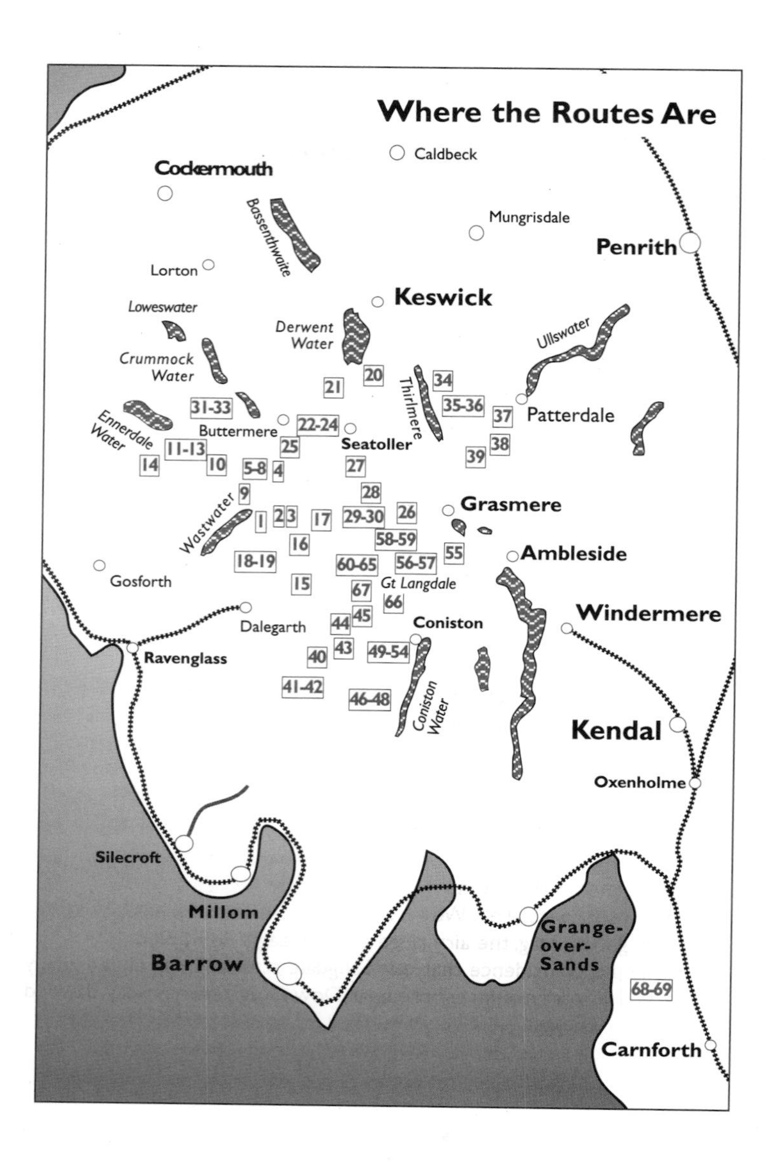

Where the Routes Are
Caldbeck
Cockermouth
Bassenthwaite
Mungrisdale
Penrith
Lorton
Keswick
Loweswater
Derwent Water
Ullswater
Crummock Water
20
21
Thirlmere
34
31-33
35-36
37
Patterdale
Ennerdale Water
Buttermere
22-24
Seatoller
38
11-13
25
39
14
10
5-8
4
27
9
28
Grasmere
Wastwater
1
2
3
17
29-30
26
58-59
16
55
Ambleside
18-19
60-65
56-57
Gosforth
15
Gt Langdale
67
66
Windermere
Dalegarth
44
45
Coniston
Ravenglass
43
49-54
40
41-42
46-48
Coniston Water
Kendal
Oxenholme
Silecroft
Millom
Barrow
Grange-over-Sands
68-69
Carnforth

Foreword

It was one of those pale-blue February days. We'd set off up Raven Crag, with a sudden moment of terror looking down through some branches to the chimneypots of the Old Dungeon Ghyll vertically below. We'd headed on up that ridge until it petered out into the grass, sidestepped to Tarn Crag, and scrambled right out of Langdale: good rock under our hands all the way up to Harrison Stickle, and the valley behind us a frosted trough of pastel greens and blues. We'd ventured into Allencrags Gill, with its cold grey rock and frozen waterfalls; and kicked our way up the soft snows of Esk Crag in noonday glare.

At the top, afternoon haze drifted along Eskdale, with Black Combe seemingly a hand's reach away across the valley.

At the dawn of the new century, rockclimbers are thrusting ever upwards and onwards (and sometimes even overhanging) - squeezing feet into shoes so special they can't be walked in; dipping fingers into chalk, and hands deep into wallets for a drapery of superbly safe jangly-danglies.

But just sometimes, at the dawn of a new century, it's amusing to look backwards into the one before last. Lakeland then was an unknown country to be explored, in big hobnailed boots, by lost mossy ways where you were your own master and, if it came to that, your own mountain rescue team as well.

Mankind is an animal that knows and loves its territory, and glories in escape routes. The mastery, or of course misstressry, of difficult terrain, gave our instinctive ancestors the sudden pounce on the enemy human or unexpected elk. We have evolved specifically to enjoy the ramble through the crag, the airy ridge and the eagle viewpoint.

So it's no coincidence that our Langdale scramble day ended, many hours later, in a cave somewhere near Dow Crag. The next day dawned more typically Lakeland. Grey cloud hung just above the dripping treetops, stirred by a listless wind. One fairly well-known Lakeland writer (not either of the present authors!) stood in Eskdale, looked up into the drizzle and decided not to bother.

A thousand feet above, Colin and I were on the southwest ridge of Coniston Old Man in golden sunlight. This ridge isn't serious scrambling. This ridge is "Colin, Colin, I've found a slightly difficult little wall over here!"

"I don't care for your little wall. My bit's got the sun on the handholds."

Behind us, the cloud surged silently over Goat's Water, and poked damp fingers into the cave where we'd just passed the night. Up at the summit we weren't saying much: just the odd "Gosh" and "Ooh". And then take extra breath for a really long speech: "I think those must be the Three Peaks".

The fully old-fashioned way is to take a length of rope and a couple of nuts, and set off up some likely-looking rockface. Most of us (including me) don't have the time for such leisurely exploring - or, indeed, the courage. In this book you'll find 69 routes, linked into the 27 hill days that two experienced climber-scramblers consider the altogether finest and most rewarding in all Lakeland. They explain how hard it is - or isn't - going to be, and where is the way that works. The book is securely bound with a sewn spine and fairly waterproof cover, so that if you do decide half way up to fling it over your shoulder and try some authentic exploring - you may well find it intact at the bottom later. Unless someone else with old-fashioned ideas of Lakeland fun has already pinched it.

Fell-walking; fell-running; the shopping in Ambleside; these are enjoyable in their different ways. But for me at least, the linked climbs and scrambles, unencumbered and impulsive, from valley floor to the shining summit - this is the most fun you can have in Lakeland with your boots on.

Ronald Turnbull

Ronald Turnbull Gatelawbridge 2003

Introduction

The Lake District has a beauty that draws pilgrims from all around the world. The building-blocks of that beauty are the rocks. And no-one knows those rocks better than the scrambler and the climber.

Two hundred years ago, pioneering tourists gazed at the crags from a safe distance; even sometimes using mirrors to set themselves at a further remove, lest the 'horrid' and 'sublime' aspects overwhelmed their senses. Yet within a century climbers were discovering that it was possible to scale the same crags, to do so in reasonable safety - and to have a huge amount of fun in the process. Every aspect of Lakeland seems, to the climber and scrambler, to be designed as if specifically for our own particular sport.

First and foremost are the crags themselves. The rocks are many times older than those of the Alps or the Himalaya. Their history is long, complex and violent. And the result is a rich mixture: rocks that lie at every possible angle; rocks of every possible colour; rocks that are uncannily smooth and rocks with more holds than you could ever use. The broad outlines of combe and crag were carved by retreating glaciers around ten thousand years ago, giving the rocks time to weather and settle: to mature, in fact, to something close to perfection.

The Lake District is where climbing, for its own sake, really began. This rock was meant to be clambered up, and you don't have to be superhuman to do it. So much of it lies at just the right angle: steep enough to be interesting, without forcing you to dangle from your hands the whole time. It is full of variety, so that you find yourself dealing with cracks, corners, chimneys, open slabs and aretes, all on the same climb. It is rough enough to give a good grip, yet rarely so rough that it will shred your fingertips; it is well-weathered, sound and reassuring. And its complexity and variety means that there are routes of all grades, with easy routes and extremely hard ones often right next to each other. This certainly adds spice for the climber of easy routes!

For the climber, whose essential medium is the foundation of the landscape, that landscape is never a mere backdrop. Climbing in the

Lakes offers all the tactile pleasure of rock, the exhilaration of climbing, and the sheer pleasure of doing so in some of the most beautiful places on Earth.

One of the things that makes the Lake District special is that the hard, high landscapes of crag and fell are never far from the softer ones of lake and dale. You climb on a gaunt mountain crag yet look out onto dense woodland, or a lake dotted with sails. You can spend all day grappling with the rocks but then, in the evening, it only takes an hour or two to get down to the comfort of the valley.

And here we must say that the Lake District not only has the best rock in the world, it also has the best pubs. You can scare yourself silly here just as effectively as you can in Patagonia or the Karakoram - although that's not quite the point of this book. But what Patagonia or the Karakoram don't give you is the chance to settle those nerves with a comforting pint a couple of hours - or even mere minutes - later.

What this book is about is making the most of what the District has to offer. By discarding the arbitrary division between scrambling and climbing, it aims to offer you some particularly satisfying days on the rocks. Best of all are the ones where you can make your way from valley floor to airy windswept summit over a full morning of scrambling and climbing, with hands on rock almost all the way up. These are the days we have called 'expeditions'. You could do our routes 15, 16 and 17 on three separate occasions. But to link the Esk Gorge, Thor's Buttress and Ill Crags into a full ascent of Scafell Pike is simply the best possible way to spend a long summer day. To climb from Langdale beside the noisy waters of Mill Gill, scramble the rough steps of Tarn Crag and then go straight up the face of Pavey Ark (Routes 56-59) can be magnificent not just in summer but also in spring or autumn, sometimes even in winter.

To concentrate solely on these floor-to-ceiling routes would be to miss out many other wonderful days. There is no rock route to the foot of Dow Crag, so that you really do have to resort to walking. But from there to the summit you can make a route that involves over 300 metres of climbing and scrambling (Routes 46-48).

There are gentler days to be enjoyed, too; pottering about on the crags which poke up from the wooded floor of the Duddon valley, for example (Routes 40-42). You could save this for when the clouds blanket the high fells, but you don't have to. Sometimes it's nice to climb in shorts and T-shirt, and it's rarely that you get that chance on Scafell Pinnacle (Route 1).

Making the most of It

Some of these routes are possible all year round. The south-facing rock of the Langdale crags stays clean, dries quickly, and is rough enough to provide reasonable friction even when wet. However, popular routes like Middlefell Buttress (Route 60) are very polished, which makes them slippery even when dry and doubly so when damp.

On the higher crags, especially the north-facing ones, the rock takes longer to dry - sometimes four or five fine days are needed even in summer - and when it is wet, it's often also greasy. Add to this the discomforts of cold hands and the clumsiness of chilled limbs, and routes can become very much harder in poor conditions. As a rough rule of thumb, a route becomes one grade more difficult when wet; but shady north-facing ones may go up by two grades. And any exposed route becomes very much more severe in high winds.

And then there are the routes that are always wet, the watercourses or gills. Gill scrambling is a very different game. Where it is actually under the stream the rock is wet, obviously, but also clean and sound. It's where it's kept damp by spray, or just by the humid atmosphere of an enclosed gill, that it becomes mossy or lichenous and almost impossibly slippery. Gills shaded by trees, even if south-facing, may need weeks of dry weather to shed their hostile aura. Some gills have a gloomy and intimidating atmosphere, while the constant noise and movement of waterfalls can be disconcerting, if not totally disorientating. It also makes it difficult to communicate with your partner.

In fact there aren't many serious gills in this book: the principal examples are Ill Gill (Route 9), and Link Cove Beck by the direct route (Route 38). Others, such as Sour Milk Gill (Route 22) and Levers Water Beck (Route 53), follow watercourses which are much more open and allow you to climb on clean rock. Even on the more difficult Low Water Beck (Route 50), the crucial sections are on open crag and not in the bed of the gill.

The climber and the environment

Climbing and scrambling bring you into a particularly close relationship with the mountain environment, and for most people this naturally fosters appreciation and care for this environment.

You may occasionally come across people, or signs, asking you to steer clear of a particular route to avoid disturbance to nesting birds. Treat all vegetation with respect - what looks like a nondescript bundle of leaves may be a rare species. Stick to the rock as much as possible - it's usually pleasanter and safer anyway. In particular, steer clear of the gorge-type gill scrambles except when water levels are low. High water is likely to force you away from the stream onto its vegetated flanks. The plant communities here are often very fragile.

Many of the problems of the wider environment are caused by the car - not just pollution and congestion but the tearing up of verges in the demand for ever more parking spaces and the destruction of hills to meet the demand for road-stone. Using public transport helps ease these pressures. It also means that you are freed to finish the day at a different place from where you began; you could traverse a ridge, instead of going up and down the same side.

Public transport is better than in most other upland areas of the UK, but it must be said that it doesn't meet all our needs. While Borrowdale has an excellent bus service, those in the other valleys simply don't continue late enough for anyone planning a long day on the fells. However, if you're planning to base yourself in a particular dale or village for several days, public transport will nearly always get you there. And if you do miss that last bus, try hitching. If you're carrying a rope, let it show; there's a good chance other climbers will stop for you.

The access information in each chapter includes public transport details. These are based on the timetable for Summer 2002. There is no reason to expect drastic changes to services, but it is always a good idea to check. Some services have actually improved in recent years, and there are grounds to hope that this trend may continue. Usable bus services to places like Wasdale Head and the Duddon Valley would be a great boon, but no single development would be more welcome than a late bus from Langdale back to Ambleside.

Using this book

In the route descriptions, the directions left and right assume you are facing the rock, unless explicitly stated otherwise. However, we'll always give further clues if there's a risk of confusion.

For routes described as climbs (i.e. pitch by pitch) the overall length is the sum of the individual pitch lengths - assuming we've done our sums correctly! For scrambles we have merely given the altitude difference between bottom and top. Some of the routes, especially some of the gills, involve lengthy sections of walking between steep bits, so an overall length measure is not very helpful.

For both climbs and scrambles we have given guide times. In the case of roped climbs these assume a party of two. For the scrambles the times assume you are climbing unroped. Some people like to climb fast; others like to savour every move. As long as you can finish before nightfall there's no harm in taking twice as long as our times.

There's a glossary at the back of the book, which should explain any unfamiliar terms.

Grading: Scrambles

Scrambling guidebooks follow the 1-2-3 system, with the addition of an 'S' (for serious) to those Grade 3 routes demanding a higher level of technical ability. This system, originated by Steve Ashton in 'Scrambles in Snowdonia', seems sufficiently well-established that many people have at least a rough idea what is meant by a Grade 1 scramble, and so on. This book will use the 1-2-3 system but without the 'S' suffix. Where a route is uncomfortably hard or exposed for a straight Grade 3 then we will grade it as a rock-climb - Moderate or even Difficult.

The best way to get the hang of any grading system is to use it. Start with Grade 1's in good conditions, and go on from there. Some people are good on slabs rather than overhangs; some are thrown by loose rock but don't mind exposure. So no grading system works exactly for everyone. And there is variation within each grade: just because you can climb one V. Diff doesn't mean you can climb them all.

Also bear in mind that the grade will increase unpredictably in poor weather. If the rock's clean and rough, a bit of wet won't make much difference, but if it's mossy or vegetated it can be a whole new ball game. A scramble up the bed of a gill may be impossible when there's a lot of water coming down. A clean but exposed ridge, on the other hand, may still be feasible in rain, but very uncomfortable in a high wind.

Very roughly, then:

Grade 1: Difficulties can normally be avoided and are not in exposed situations. Route-finding is pretty straightforward. Escape sideways is usually possible. A Grade 1 could be attempted, given good conditions, by a confident fell-walker: examples are Jack's Rake on Pavey Ark and Sharp Edge on Blencathra.

Grade 2: More difficult and committing situations will be found, and route-finding may require judgment. Loose rock may also require careful assessment. Inexperienced parties would carry a rope, even if it might not be used.

Grade 3: Can involve difficult moves, sometimes on dubious rock or in exposed situations. Route-finding may be quite complicated. A rope would be used by all but the most experienced.

Grading: Rock climbs

The British grading system for rock-climbs has a long history, but can be confusing for the uninitiated. 'Easy' has effectively disappeared from the climbing guide books - many of those routes now appear as scrambles. So far as we are concerned, as with the scrambles, there are just three grades to bother about. Learn to say 'Mod', 'Diff' and 'V. Diff' if you want to sound like a climber!

Moderate: require no particular technical skill, and a beginner could expect to achieve them climbing second on the rope. They still do require proper ropework, and confidence. They can be steep, exposed and scary! Crescent Climb (Route 58) is a perfect example.

Difficult: steeper rock, smaller holds, but still within the capacity of a beginner given a lot of confidence and a good leader. Good examples are Middlefell Buttress (Route 60) and 'C' Ordinary (Route 46).

Very Difficult: Some V. Diffs involve short overhanging sections. Although these will always have good holds, they still demand arm strength. Others require quite delicate climbing on small holds. Familiarity with basic technical moves such as back-and-foot and hand-jamming also helps. Routes like Trinity Slabs (Route 42) or Scout Crag Route 1 (our Route 55) offer a reasonable introduction to V. Diff climbing.

We shall occasionally mention harder climbs alongside our routes. The system extends through Severe to Very Severe (VS) and then into the Extreme bracket. If you have tackled in good style the hardest routes in this book - Oxford and Cambridge Direct (Route 33), Bowfell Buttress (Route 67) and Ash Tree Slabs (Route 61) - then a Mild Severe would be a logical next step.

Maps and diagrams

We have included basic location and approach route maps in addition to 3d panoramas, crag drawings and crag photographs. These should be used in conjunction with good maps, either from the Ordnance Survey or from Harvey. Although, for valley walkers the OS Explorer/ Outdoor Leisure maps have the edge (they show field boundaries), for more legible crag detail and contour lines, Harvey are superior. In their 1:25 000 Superwalker series, the Lake District is divided into six maps: Lakeland North, South, East, West, West and South East. See their website www.harveymaps.co.uk.

Ordnance Survey Explorer maps are the same scale and divide the Lake Distict into four, namely OL4 to OL 7 (NW, NE, SW, SE)

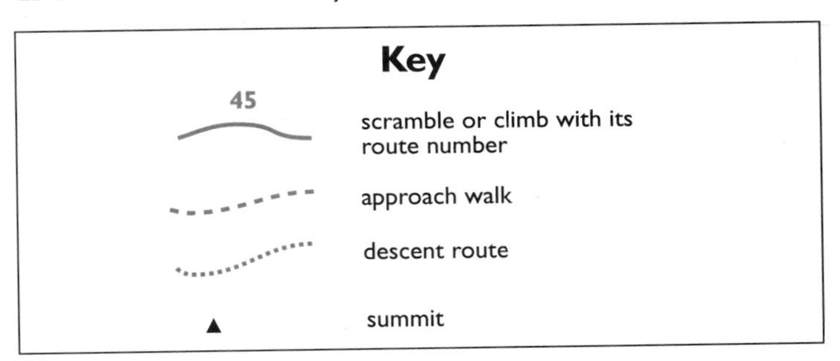

Getting started

Most people move into scrambling as a natural progression from walking. Natural indeed - children are eager and uninhibited climbers, whether on wobbly bookcases, trees, or the rocks behind the beach. Unfortunately, most of us have to learn to climb all over again, much more laboriously, as adults.

Once you find that Striding Edge and Jack's Rake are enjoyable rather than terrifying, it's natural to look around for other places where you need to use hands as well as feet, where you can feel the bones of Lakeland under your fingertips. And perhaps, as a bonus, escape the

Bernie Carter scrambling on Tarn Crag, Langdale (Route 57). Note the balanced posture as well as the use of approach shoes, and a well-fitting rucksack which remains stable when climbing.

crowds. I did once get Striding Edge to myself, but it was before breakfast-time.

Many people learn scrambling without ever being taught, and most of them end up as competent and safe scramblers. However, going on a course will certainly speed up this learning process, and may prevent you developing bad - and potentially dangerous - habits. See the chapter Exploring Further, at the back of the book, for more details.

Still, the time-honoured way to get scrambling is simply by going out and doing it. In this case the best advice is obvious: start with easy stuff.

Begin, then, with a Grade I in good conditions. Two good examples are The Bell (Route 49) and Lever's Water Beck (Route 53), both at Coniston. Another good one, if you stick to the easy ways, is Sour Milk Gill (Route 22) in Borrowdale. As a walker you may have already done Jack's Rake or Sharp Edge, both counted as scrambles. Other Grade I's, like those in this book, will be less well-trodden - and therefore less obvious - and you're much more likely to be on your own. There may be odd bits of dodgy rock. You will have to decide for yourself on the safety, and possibility, of every step.

However accurate the guide-book's description may be, it still takes a little experience to tie it in with the mass of rock in front of you. Keep sight of the bigger picture - the overall line of the route - rather than just following the most tempting holds, which may lead into a blind alley. Such experience builds up naturally. So does the experience to spot when a particular flake of rock has worked loose, or to know whether your boot will really stick on that slab. And so, crucially, does the experience to know when to turn back, or slope off to the side. On many of the easier scrambles it's possible to escape onto easier ground without having to climb all the way back down.

Having successfully negotiated a few Grade 1's, you might move up to a Grade 2. Good 'starter' Grade 2's include Little Blake Rigg (Route 44) or Tarn Crag East Rib (Route 57). You may find it equally interesting to try the Grade 1's in less good conditions.

As you move up the grades, you start to wonder about the point where the grade numbers change to names... The difference between scrambling and climbing is not so much the routes being tackled as the way you tackle them. Climbing involves a rope, and a clearly defined route. And from ground level, that route probably looks thoroughly alarming and impossibly vertical.

Suppose, then, that you've been scrambling Grade 2 and Grade 3 and you're curious about the next step. Just what is it that you might be getting into?

There are people who think that climbing is some form of Indian Rope Trick. It isn't. In normal climbing, the aim is never to put any weight on the rope. It and all the hardware are used only for protection - not to stop you from falling off, but to stop you from hurting yourself if you do. Rock-climbing requires a team of at least two. The essential principle is that only one member of the team is moving at a time, while the other is firmly belayed to the rock.

Clearly the second person up isn't going to fall at all - at worst, they may swing sideways. However, the rope also secures the first person up a given section or pitch; that person is referred to, reasonably enough, as the leader. She places running belays at intervals for protection. These can be rope loops called slings placed over spikes of rock or threaded behind chockstones. At each of these runners the rope runs through a karabiner (a spring-loaded clip or snap-link).

With a runner in place every few metres, even if the leader does fall, she isn't going to fall far. It's not the falling that hurts, it's the stopping at the bottom - but the stretchiness of a climbing rope makes even this reasonably comfortable.

Climbing will take you onto steeper - and often cleaner - rock. You will notice more exposure - the jargon word for big drops. Climbing looks a great deal more scary than scrambling. Oddly, once you learn to have confidence in the rope, it may feel considerably less so. And provided the rope is being used properly, it is actually a great deal safer than any ropeless scramble. If you understand the principles of belaying and ropework, can place secure protection, and know your own limits, then climbing on Lakeland crags is a safe sport. And the mountain rescue statistics bear this out.

Onwards and upwards

So what does it take to move from scrambler to rock rat?

Well, more gear, for a start. And that means not just getting the gear but learning how to use it. The legendary Joe Brown really did start off with his mother's washing line. Fortunately, however, he was soon taken in tow by climbers who knew what a real rope looked like, and how to use it. Otherwise one of the greatest of all British climbers might have had a much shorter career.

Climbing is more complex than scrambling. The quick and safe way to learn is from an experienced climber, probably on a course or through a club. An indoor climbing wall is a great place to pick up the skills of movement on rock, but won't teach you about route-finding, placing protection, or setting up safe belays. It is, however, a good way to meet people who can teach you these things.

You could also learn from books (though it's beyond the scope of this one) or videos, though this is neither as effective nor as enjoyable. However good the book, a 'teach yourself' approach also entails a degree of trial and error - and the consequences of error can be dire. Many climbers - including both the authors of this book - started this way, but we spent a lot of time top-roping on small crags before attempting to lead anything. Learning from a seasoned climber would have been both quicker and safer.

Another difference between climbing and scrambling is that climbing takes a lot longer. This is partly because only one person moves at a time, partly because of the need to place protection. There's often a third reason. The higher level of safety means that a roped climber can venture onto steeper rock, rock with fewer or smaller holds, rock where the moves are more strenuous or more intricate.

To some people this physical side is the be-all and end-all of climbing. They enjoy 'sport climbs', climbing walls, and small boulders. On our sort of climbs it is just one part - albeit an important one - of the all-round experience. Placing protection properly, both for safety and so the rope runs freely, is a gratifying skill. So is 'reading the rock', which on the larger scale helps you stay on the right route. On the smaller scale, it's surprising how often a sidestep, or just a look around, can turn an apparently impossible move into something quite reasonable.

Judith Brown leading, belayed by Maggie Ingram, on Oliverson's Variation, Gimmer Crag (Route 62). Note the running belay, placed at the first opportunity.

Moving up over a big drop, secure and in control, is a great feeling. So is sitting on a small ledge, feet dangling, firmly belayed, while your partner takes their turn to untangle the intricacies of a pitch. And so is arriving at the top, stepping onto level ground again as your horizon suddenly expands from a few metres of rock to distant fells and the afternoon light on the Irish Sea.

Roped scrambling

According to our earlier definition, if it's got a rope on then it's a rock-climb and so there's no such thing as roped scrambling. In fact many people will start wishing for a rope on the Grade 3 scrambles. And, of course, Grade 2 in good conditions may become very much harder in bad. If you want a rope, never be afraid to say so, even if there are others romping around quite happily unroped. Better embarrassed than hurt.

A short rope (maybe 25m) will get a group out of most situations on most scrambles. While it is often possible to arrange belays with nothing more than the rope itself, it expands your options greatly if you carry a few slings and karabiners too, maybe even one or two nuts. Simply carrying the gear is no use unless at least one member of the party knows how to use it. As a minimum they should know how to tie onto the rope, how to belay from a fixed stance and how to set up a running belay. Knowledge of a simple abseil technique would be a bonus. These techniques are part of any scrambling course. These base-level skills could be acquired from a book, but must then be thoroughly practised on safe ground before they're needed.

When one member of a group is carrying a rope, it is important for all to keep in contact. It's no good one of you suddenly deciding you'd like the rope on when it's already out of sight beyond the hard bit. It can be even worse if you're the one out in front, you suddenly feel insecure, and the rope's with someone twenty metres below. The best person to carry the rope is the one who's least likely to need it i.e. the most experienced member. And as a rule they should go first, but make sure not to get too far ahead.

Climbing together

Between pitched climbing and unroped climbing, there is a third way. Few British climbers, other than Alpine veterans, seem to understand anything about the art called moving together. This is a shame, because moving together, while not as safe as pitched climbing, does provide much greater security than unroped climbing, yet allows a party to move almost as fast.

Moving together has fairly limited application in the Lakes, but is still worth knowing about. If you do have aspirations to the Alps, where reasonable speed is a crucial element in safety, it is good to get some practice in. The essence is that two (or more) climbers are roped together, but without fixed belays. A typical rope length between climbers is 15m or so. On easy ground you simply pick up coils of slack rope and carry them in one hand. As things get more serious, the coils are released and the leader places running belays at intervals. Sometimes a natural spike or flake of rock will act as a runner without any additional gear. The climbers continue to move together, but should not take coils in hand, and should adjust their pace to prevent any slack rope forming between them - this takes practice. If things get tougher still, it takes only moments for the second to take a secure belay and convert moving together into full-dress roped climbing.

Equipment

Footwear

On scrambles, it is usual to climb in the boots you have walked up in. Many people will be happy climbing Diffs and V.Diffs in boots, too. The best ones for climbing and scrambling are fairly light: it doesn't matter how good the footholds are if you can't lift your feet onto them! A good fit is absolutely essential: a boot that wobbles or flops around is uncomfortable to walk in, but dangerous for climbing. Soles should not be too bendy and should have crisp, more or less right-angled, edges. Trendy rounded bumps and knobbles are not helpful on small holds.

Ordinary trainers, with their thick spongy soles, are a poor choice for scrambling and climbing. Many people have taken to 'approach shoes' for scrambling and easy climbs. These are basically a cross between trainers and boots. Again, look for a good fit, reasonable support (especially lateral support) and a sensible sole.

Specialised rock boots are a pleasure to climb in. However, you can't walk up to the crag in them; and they are not essential for any of the routes in this book. Many scrambles, and a few of the climbs, involve sections of steep grass between the rocky bits. This can feel very insecure in rock-boots, especially if damp.

In damp, greasy conditions, any rubber sole can feel insecure. Bringing back nailed boots might be a good idea, except that they damage the rock. Wearing socks over the top of your boots is a time-honoured dodge that really works in these conditions. It's a lot easier to get socks over rock boots than it is to stretch them over walking boots. Wool has the best friction; synthetics like Nylon are comparatively slippery.

Clothing:

Whatever you wear for walking should be suitable, but aim for freedom of movement - a waist-length rather than knee-length jacket, for example. Two or three thin layers are more versatile than one thick one.

Scrambling, with its fairly continuous movement, will usually keep you warm. Rock-climbing, however, involves waiting around on stances. Change to something warmer before you start, rather than on that small ledge above the first pitch.

Hats and gloves make a big difference, too, though if you're going to climb bare-handed - which is advisable on all but the easiest scrambles - you should let your hands acclimatise to the temperature before you start on the rock. If it's really too cold to walk up bare-handed, is it going to be too cold to climb?

Rucksacks

Many of the trips in this book involve a linked sequence of routes. Here you will be climbing with your rucksack, rather than leaving it at the foot of the crag. This takes getting used to, but the design of the sack can make a big difference.

Look for a slim sack, perhaps a teardrop shape which allows most of the weight to be carried low. A narrow profile at shoulder level allows

Bernie Carter on Arrowhead Ridge, Great Gable (Route 8). The use of double ropes gives extra protection to the second here

free arm movement. The ideal sack will be small, without side-pockets and without excessively padded shoulder straps, which can impede arm movement. Compression straps that allow you to reduce the volume of the sack will make it more stable after you've taken out the climbing gear.

The waist belt may interfere with a climbing harness, in which case the belt should be strapped back out of the way - don't leave it flapping.

Technical gear

Climbing harnesses do make life easier; they're convenient when belaying and give you somewhere to carry the nuts and runners. They only become essential when you're on steep rock, where a fall could leave you hanging more or less free. In such situations the traditional method of simply tying the rope around your waist is dangerous. However, there are very few places on the climbs in this book where this situation could occur. Nevertheless, wearing a harness on the roped climbs is a very good idea.

A selection of nuts is usually carried, though on the routes in this book it is unnecessary to burden yourself with micro sizes or expensive camming devices. Six or eight nuts will suffice, perhaps a few more on the hardest routes in the book. However, it is well worth taking several slings, as flakes, spikes and chockstones are common on these easier Lakeland climbs.

Helmets

Modern helmets are lighter, more comfortable and better-looking than ever before. There seems little excuse for not wearing one wherever there's a risk either of falling off or of anything else falling off on top of you from above. This includes the steeper scrambles, where loose rocks are not unlikely, as well as rock climbs.

A cautionary note

Of course, the descriptions and diagrams in this book are as clear as they can possibly be, but experience still helps in reading the rock. The introduction to each route will point out routes which are more than usually devious, where protection is less than generous, stances less than large.

This and other guidebooks sometimes refer to rock being 'perfect',

Approach to the Sour Milk Gill scramble Borrowdale, Gillercombe Expedition

'impeccable' and so on. Sadly nothing in life is ever perfect, not even Bowfell Buttress. Much of the rock in the Lake District is superb, but occasional loose holds can occur even on well-used routes. Learn to assess the rock first visually and also by testing suspect holds before committing to them. Some holds will actually move, others will sound hollow when tapped.

If rock does seem loose, distribute your weight. The traditional advice is to maintain three points of contact but this should really be three points of support. Sometimes holds that won't stand a direct pull can be pushed instead.

In some senses, the harder scrambles can actually be harder than the rock climbs. They can certainly feel more serious. On the South-east face of Ill Crags, the route is not laid down and marked in advance, and every man and woman up it is an explorer. The finding of a safe and feasible route is down to your own judgment, with potentially severe penalties for getting it wrong.

And this is the point of any adventurous activity, surely: that it makes you rely on yourself. Certainly in rock-climbing and scrambling you are ultimately responsible for your own safety. None of the routes in this book is unduly dangerous - if you approach it sensibly. If you don't, then all of the routes in this book are potentially dangerous - and so is everything else in life.

Enough of the sombre stuff. There is nothing better than scrambling and climbing, and no better place than the Lake District to do it. Take care - but have fun!

Jon Sparks
Lancaster 2003

Judith Brown
Great Broughton 2003

Wasdale Ennerdale and Eskdale

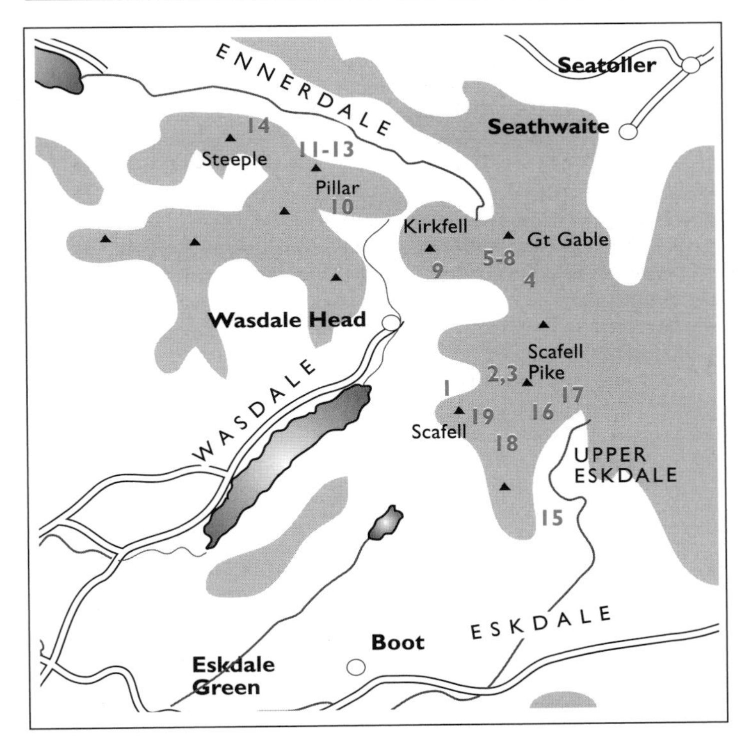

The mountain crags of Wasdale – Pillar, Scafell and the Napes of Gable – are the birthplace of British rock climbing. The exact location is sometimes given as the Wasdale Head Inn, base for the early explorers in the days when mountaineers were gentlemen of independent means. Today, climbers are more likely to rough it, but the attraction of discussing routes, both real and imagined, over a pint of Gable Bitter remains as strong as ever.

The actual time of birth has been subject to debate – Cumberland shepherds had been scrambling over the fells for centuries rescuing cragfast sheep. Climbing and scrambling as we currently mean it is undertaken for no purpose other than personal pleasure – although in the midst of a cold, wet and potentially dangerous ascent it is easy to forget that we are doing this for fun!

The first of today's rock-climbs to be recorded in writing was Broad Stand, which was descended by the poet Coleridge in 1802. His description will be recognised by many of today's climbers when faced with the descent from their first ever climb on Scafell: '....the ledge below was so exceedingly narrow, that if I dropt down upon it I must of necessity have fallen backwards and of course killed myself.'

As this was a descent, perhaps it doesn't count. In that case, the title of first rock-climber belongs to the shepherd John Atkinson, who climbed Pillar Rock by what is now called the Old West Route in 1826. His feat was recorded in the The Cumberland Paquet and Wares Whitehaven Advertiser.

It was not until late in the century that rock climbing began to develop as a defined sport. The 1880s saw much exploration in the area, with the key event being the soloing of Napes Needle by Haskett-Smith in 1886. This route has been popular ever since, and the high polish imparted by over a century of thrutches has increased its grade to Hard Severe, rather ironically putting it outside the scope of this book.

When you climb the routes described here you will have the satisfaction of following in the footsteps (and hand holds) of the great pioneers such as O.G. Jones, the Abraham Brothers and Cecil Slingsby. As you don your modern gear, pause to admire those who made these routes with no 'illegitimate means', and, moreover, no guide book.

But for a full-on nineteenth-century experience, you need to leave most of that modern gear at home, and attack Scafell or Scafell Pike from the back. You'll find solitude, moss on the rocks, and routes requiring actual exploration, when you tackle one of the scrambling expeditions in Upper Eskdale.

Access

Wasdale is still one of the more remote parts of the Lake District. Access is by a scenic single-track road following the lake shore. Caravans are not permitted on this road. There is adequate parking at the National Trust Campsite and on the Green at Wasdale Head.

Public transport, unfortunately, is extremely limited. Gosforth Taxis run morning and evening minibus services on Thursdays, Saturdays and Sundays; their pick-up is at Seascale station. These will not run if there are no pre-booked passengers: phone 019467 25308 not later than 6pm the previous day. Other options for those without cars, apart from hitching, involve a substantial walk, either from Boot in Eskdale, or from Seatoller in Borrowdale. Boot can be reached via the 'Laal Ratty' narrow-gauge railway (see below), and the walk to Wasdale Head is about 7km with 300m of ascent via the Old Corpse Road past Burnmoor Tarn. This is rough and wet in places but not too steep. The route from Borrowdale is a similar distance but involves a steeper climb over Sty Head; however, Borrowdale has much better access by public transport.

Amenities

Wasdale Head today has accommodation to suit every pocket, though demand can exceed supply. The Wasdale Head Inn still offers superb amenities, including self-catering apartments and a campsite and climbing shop. For those who prefer a sobering walk before falling into their sleeping bag, there is a large, well-appointed National Trust campsite at the head of the lake, 1km down-valley from the Inn. More pubs, B&B accommodation, etc, are found in the gentler scenery down the valley. There is a youth hostel at Wasdale Hall, near the foot of the lake, a camping barn at Murt, and pubs at Nether Wasdale and Santon Bridge.

Upper Eskdale

The best village bases are Eskdale Green, where there is a youth hostel as well as the George IV pub, and Boot, which has two pubs and campsites. The nearest accommodation and refreshment point to Brotherilkeld is the Woolpack Inn. There are B&Bs scattered throughout the valley. Access by car is easiest from the A595 in the west. This is the only route for those towing caravans. A minor road, with superb views, crosses the fells from Ulpha in the Duddon valley. The most direct approach from the central Lakes, though often a slow one, is via the very steep and narrow Wrynose and Hardknott passes.

Scafell Crag Day

130m climbing (including Broad Stand descent): 80m scrambling: up to V.Diff

Scafell offers some of the highest, longest routes in England. Scafell Crag, and particularly its East Buttress, is famous for hard, steep and committing

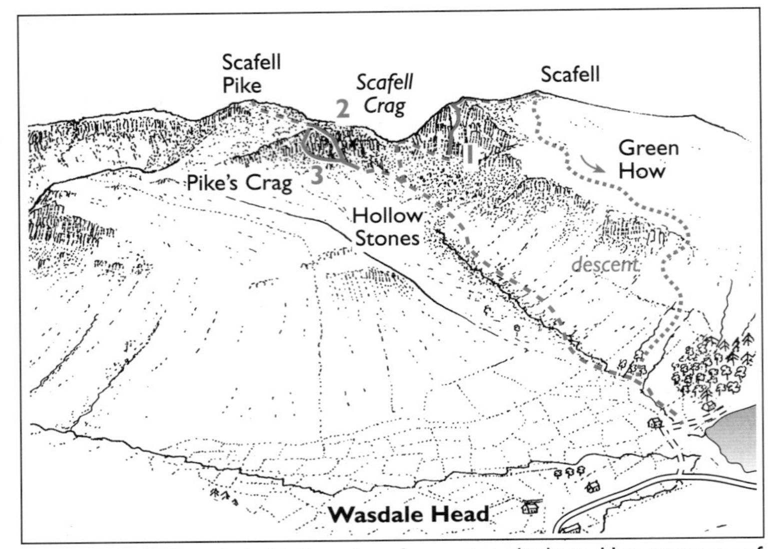

routes. It is an intimidating place for novice climbers. However, one of the original pioneering routes on the crag makes its way through these difficulties and splendours at a considerably lower grade, to arrive, superbly, on the very summit of Scafell Pinnacle.

Rock-climbing guides to the crag describe some other recommended routes at the V.Diff standard. Due to the lack of traffic in recent years, not to mention the lack of sunshine, the star-ratings, along with the routes themselves, must now be regarded as traditional. Better to return to climb the great routes at Hard Severe, Very Severe and above.

Approach

The shortest way is from Wasdale via Hollow Stones. From the National Trust car park near the big campsite, follow the track past Brackenclose house, and cross the stream via a bridge. The path now leads up the left bank of the stream, which it eventually crosses via a boulder hop. The very popular path has been largely paved to reduce erosion. In the 'Three Peaks' season, this is not a quiet walk, but the climber can feel a smug satisfaction from the fact that the hordes will soon be left behind.

The path continues up the hillside to Hollow Stones. At a cairn, fork right, leaving the main track, to cross the broad grassy area of Hollow Stones, heading for the bottom of a huge scree gully. Pick up the paved path again to a truck-sized boulder, then follow the loose and badly eroded path up scree and through reddish rocks to emerge on the col of Mickledore. From here the track divides to go left (north-eastwards) to Scafell Pike, down (south-west) to Eskdale passing under the East Buttress, or right (west) to Scafell Main Crag. Follow this last option. The path is a little rocky to start with, becoming more grassy lower down before disappearing into the rock cleft that is the start of Lord's Rake. Stop before this point to get your bearings. This is a steep ascent, so allow about 2 hours from Wasdale.

From the vantage point of the path, it is worthwhile identifying the key features of the crag. There are two steep gully clefts rising above the path. The left one is Moss Gill, to the left of which is the main sweep of Central Buttress (look out for the leftwards slanting, steep and narrow slab of the classic Very Severe climb, Botterill's Slab). The right cleft is Steep Gill. To the right of Steep Gill, lying between it and Deep Gill, is Scafell Pinnacle, which has two tops, Low Man and High Man.

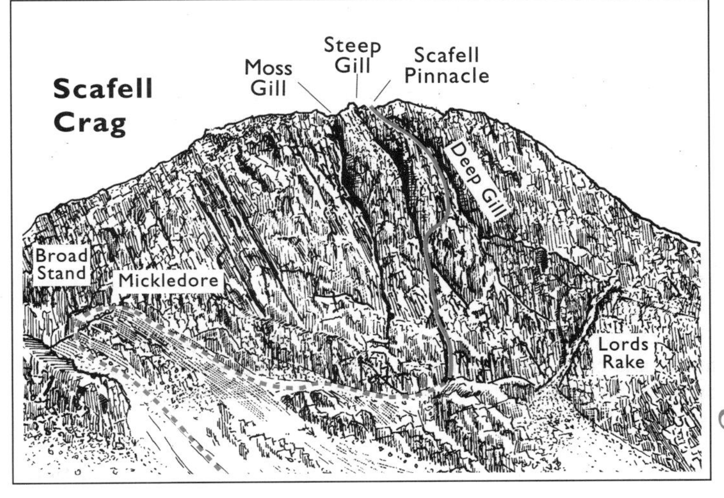

1. SLINGSBY'S ROUTE (High Man via Steep Gill and Slingsby's Chimney in older guides) 107m V.Diff

Guide time 1 hour 45 minutes

The grade applies to the start of Pitch 3 only (Slingsby's Chimney). The rest of the route is Moderate with a move or two of Diff. This fine classic route has sharply contrasting pitches, breathtaking views and a finish right on the summit of Scafell Pinnacle. Like most routes on Scafell, it needs a few days to dry out after wet weather. A party including Cecil Slingsby and the legendary Haskett-Smith first climbed the route in 1888.

Start on the Lord's Rake path, a couple of metres to left of the aforementioned rock cleft. Scramble up grass terraces and short rock ledges, trending right towards the foot of Steep Gill. Climb up the gill, which is easy, but with much loose rock. Keep in the bed of the main gully until just below the point where it narrows and steepens, becoming enclosed, dark and gorge-like. Here the route will break out of the gully to the right. (65m from the Lord's Rake path.)

1. (22m) Take to the right wall of the gully. Scramble over easy rocks and ledges to reach a feature called the Crevasse, the meaning of which becomes obvious when you see it! Belay at its left-hand end.

2. (12m) Make a short traverse to the right along the lip of the Crevasse, then make a very awkward step across it and climb a short slab to the foot of Slingsby's Chimney.

3. (40m) Climb the undercut chimney, via a couple of difficult moves, which may be executed either gymnastically or elegantly. Once you are upright again the standard eases noticeably. Continue up the chimney, and scramble to the top of Low Man (the lower, preliminary top of Scafell Pinnacle).

4. (33m) Ascend the photogenic Knife-Edge Arete, then climb along the crest to High Man, the summit of Scafell Pinnacle. Sling belays are a couple of metres before the cairn.

High Man is a true pinnacle, detached from the main massif on all sides.

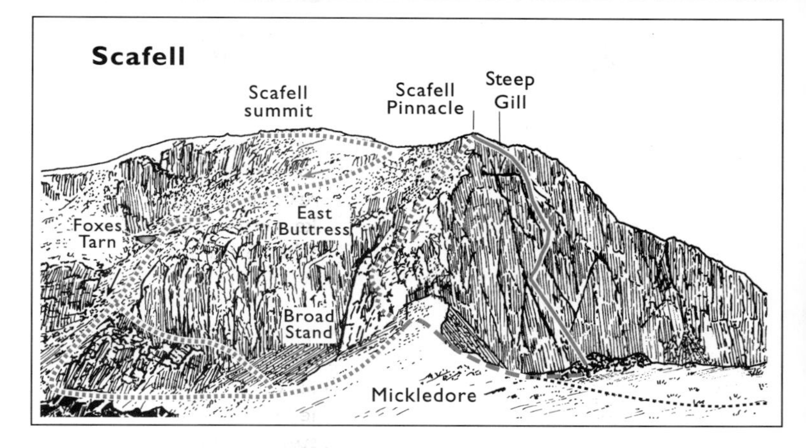

From here to the stony summit plateau is a very short distance and the scrambling is not hard, but it is sensible to leave a rope on. From High Man, drop off to the east, climbing down a moderate slab for about 10m to a bridge crossing of a narrow gully (Jordan Gap).

The next outcrop is called Pisgah. It is skirted on the right on a faint grassy path moving slightly upwards until a junction with a main track is met (roughly 20m).

And Now? From here, you can descend north-east back to Mickledore via the notorious Broad Stand (see below) or to the path below the main crag via Deep Gill and Lord's Rake. At the time of writing, the National Trust is advising walkers to avoid Lord's Rake due to a loose boulder. However, this is soon expected to slide off down the gully. The longest, but easiest, alternative is by Foxes' Tarn. Those who've done the climb with sacks can head south-west to the summit of Scafell (about 5 minutes) whence it is possible to descend to Wasdale via Green How.

Broad Stand is not for the faint hearted and its short but fierce problem is worse for those below average stature. The way to it is difficult to locate unless on a busy climbing day when there will be a stream of climbers descending to it. Follow a rough, faint track northeast on scree ledges and some easy scrambling to find the gully of Mickledore Chimney (which runs down northeast). Head down on the rim of this, on its left, on well-worn scrambling and little ledges, until you see the wide, sloping shelf (Broad Stand proper) on the left. Mickledore is now visible below and left. Move left along the ledge to a sprawling cairn. Below this a well-used groove has a chockstone belay near its top - but an abseil is not recommended due to the quantity of loose rock lying around. The groove leads down to the top of a steep 3m wall. This is descended by facing in and using holds on its top or in the crack on its right. Tall people can get their toes to the sloping platform below. Short people cannot. Someone already on the platform can help in these cases.

From the platform, climb down and round to the left for a few well polished metres to another platform. This is escaped through a narrow cleft (Fat Man's Agony) shiny with the squeeze of numerous bodies, to emerge on the screes just below Mickledore.

Pikes Crag Day

204m climbing, up to V Diff - see outline sketch on page 30

Pikes Crag forms the west-facing ramparts of the rock wall that surrounds the approach to Mickledore. The routes described are both on Pulpit Rock, the central mass of Pikes Crag. Catching the sun for much of the day and offering several good rock climbs in the lower grades, it has a much friendlier ambience than the other Scafell crags. The rock is fairly clean and dries more quickly than the neighbouring crags, but it is still best reserved for a dry summer day.

Approach from Wasdale's National Trust car park, via the main path up Brown Tongue towards Mickledore. As you reach Hollow Stones the crag appears due east. At the point where the path passes to right of a truck-size boulder, bear off left and strike up directly to the foot of the crag. About 1 1/2 hours from the car park.

2. Grooved Arete 112m V. Diff

Guide time 2 1/2 to 3 hours, including initial scrambling.

This outing has plenty of good, traditional protection and belays (slings and hexes in abundance) a good line, varied climbing and superb views of Scafell Crag. First climbed in 1924.

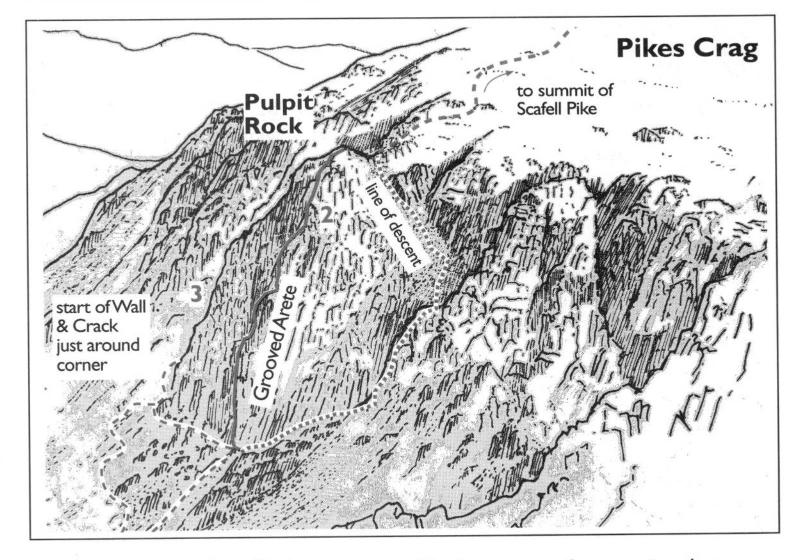

From the approach walk the most notable feature on the crag is a long groove. The arete to its left is interrupted low down by an imposing overhang. The route starts in the lower reaches of the groove but breaks out left below the overhang and then attempts to climb the arete above it.

Start by scrambling through vegetated, broken rock, aiming for the overhang. A good stance and belays are available part-way, but it is possible to scramble unroped right to the start of the groove, directly below the overhang, where the first climbing pitch begins.

1. (15m) Climb a crack, at the right edge of a steep slab, which runs up to the left of the overhang. Climb this until small but good holds lead you leftwards onto the arete. Climb this, and move up to a grass ledge a little higher than the overhang, to belay in the chimney behind.

2. (27m) Climb the chimney, then continue up a broken groove. Move rightwards over vegetated ledges to a stance at the bottom of a square-cut corner.

3. (22m) Climb the crack in the corner for about 18m until it is possible to make a short traverse right to a large block which stands out on the edge.

4. (20m) Climb the slabs and blocks above, moving slightly leftwards to start, but quickly moving back right to the arete. Climb up a series of blocks and ledges to a stance overlooking the edge, with good thread belays.

5. (13m) Move up from the stance and step left across the top of a corner. Climb up left to a chimney to left of a huge block. Climb the chimney to the enormous chockstone which caps it. Belay on the chockstone.

6. (15m) From the top of the chockstone, follow an easy ledge down to the left to regain the slabby front of the buttress. Climb this directly to the summit of Pulpit Rock.

Next: You could continue straight to the summit of Scafell Pike, or return to the foot of the crag, possibly to take in a second route. Descent details after the next route.

3. Wall & Crack Climb 92m V. Diff

Guide time 2 - 2 1/2 hours, including the initial scramble.

This is a more technical climb than the previous route, alternating delicate and bold wall climbing with strenuous crack lines. It is also less easy to protect, but has excellent stances and an obvious line. Although some polish attests to previous popularity, the rock is not as clean as in the past and dry conditions are recommended for the ascent. First climbed in 1924 by a party led by H Kelly, one of the district's great pioneers between the wars.

Start: The route takes the well-defined left-hand ridge of Pulpit Rock. Scramble up broken rock and steep turf to reach the abrupt rise of clean rock at the base of the ridge.

1. (12m) Start at the foot of the ridge and climb it on good holds until stopped by a steep wall above an obvious stance.

2. (10m) The steep wall has a fine crack running its full height. This crack provides placement for nuts and hexes to protect the elegant climbing to a ledge at the foot of a wide vertical crack.

3. (17m) Depending upon body mass, bravery and the amount of green present, it may be both possible and exciting to ascend the crack, which is almost a narrow chimney. A more aesthetic approach is to climb the face on the right of the crack. This requires a very bold move to get established, but rapidly leads onto positive holds. Either option brings you to a short rock staircase, which is climbed to a terrace.

4. (12m) From the terrace climb the wall above, starting at its right-hand side up a crack, and moving leftwards on improving holds to a ledge.

5. (12m) The crack above can be protected with large nuts, and succumbs to a mixed approach of jamming, layaways, and precise footwork. It rises in three steps to a terrace.

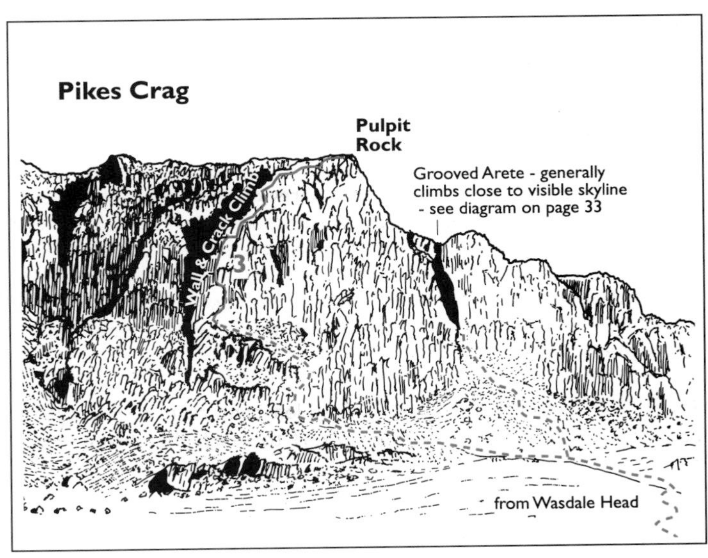

6. (12m) From here a delicate sequence of rock steps, with sparse protection, leads to the foot of a prominent crack. Belay below this.

7. (17m) Climb the crack or the wall on its left, or a combination of the two, until an excellent thread runner is gained. A few metres of easier climbing lead to belays where the overall angle of the ridge eases off. Scramble up the easier upper section of the ridge to the summit of Pulpit Rock.

Descent: Getting off the summit of Pulpit Rock requires some scrambling, the easiest line being a little to the right as you look down on the neck connecting to the mountain behind. This leads naturally to the head of the gully. The neck also leads out onto easy, but very rough, slopes below the summit of Scafell Pike.

It is important to choose the correct gully for descent. Although it looks unlikely, this is the one that drops down almost immediately to your right (with your back to Wasdale). It may be advisable to use a rope on this descent, particularly in mist, when it is easy to stray off route. The gully is very loose and care is needed. Keep to the right of the dividing rock rib until faced with an unpleasant drop, then move onto the rib itself and climb down it into the bed of the gully. Continue over loose scree to the base of the crag.

If the ground is unknown, allow up to an hour to negotiate it safely.

Great Gable Crag Day

380m climbing, up to V. Diff

The Napes offers long routes of Alpine character in a rockscape of sweeping ridges and steep buttresses. Here you will find two of the most photographed monoliths in Lakeland – Sphinx Rock and Napes Needle. Most of the ridges are of reasonable grade, and attracted the Victorian pioneers of British mountaineering – to climb here is to be part of that tradition. While it is no longer possible to climb Napes Needle without stepping up a couple of notches in grade, you will enjoy great views of that icon of British climbing.

Kern Knotts, though very small, offers another gem of traditional climbing. It can be easily incorporated when approaching the Napes

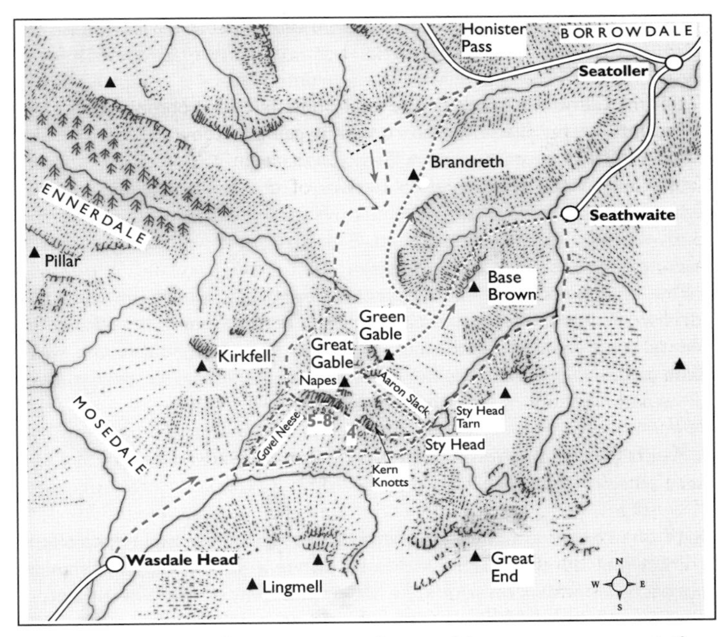

from Sty Head. All the routes are clean and have a sunny aspect; they dry quickly, while a sprinkling of mosture does not up the grade unduly.

Approaches

The time-honoured approach is from Wasdale Head, with the Napes crags clearly in sight for most of the way. Climb straight up the grindingly steep ridge of Gavel Neese and then traverse right to the Napes crags.

A gentler approach, which allows Kern Knotts to be included, is via Sty Head. As you reach Sty Head pass (southwest of Styhead Tarn), an obvious path strikes northeast up the fellside - the direct route for Gable. Take a less steep path to the left of this, behind the stretcher box. Head eastwards and very slightly uphill over boggy ground, following a faint traverse path which becomes more definite as you approach Kern Knotts (about 1 hour 40 minutes). The onward path from Kern Knotts to the Napes (another 30 min) is well worn.

The quickest approach to the Napes is from the car park at Honister Youth Hostel. The Honister Rambler bus doesn't run late enough for a day-trip to the Napes. It is, however, extremely useful if you plan a night or two at the youth hostel.

From Honister, take the main tramway path, striking out left from its top to follow poor paths below Grey Knotts and Brandreth. Pass under Gable Crag to the Beck Head col between Gable and Kirk Fell. Descend slightly through the col, until a faint traverse line contouring the screes south-westwards can be followed. Eventually this will bring you out below the Napes (about 1 1/2 hours).

The only feasible day-trip approach by public transport uses the Borrowdale Rambler service to Seatoller, from where it is about a 20 minute road walk to Seathwaite (terminus for cars). Follow the well-made path to Styhead Tarn, and the route to Kern Knotts given above. Allow a good 2 hours for this approach.

4. Kern Knotts West Chimney 30m V. Diff

Guide time 1/2 hour

More of a corner crack than a chimney, this well-protected route offers a direct line up the crag. It yields to either a strenuous or a nimble approach, depending on your style and the amount of damp in the crack! The first ascent in 1897 was led by the famous O G Jones ('the Only Genuine Jones').

Kern Knotts is a small, steep crag which faces south and west. This aspect, plus the general cleanness of the rock, means that, for a such high crag, it is quick to dry after rain.

Start: Coming from Sty Head, the westerly aspect is encountered first, identified by two big cracks running almost the height of the crag (Kern Knotts Crack and Innominate Crack, both VS). Carry on over boulders to the southerly face. The big, obvious chimney is Kern Knotts Chimney (Hard Severe). Immediately to the left of this is an area of steep rock, bounded on its left hand side by a second, very narrow chimney (or very wide crack!) This is Kern Knotts West Chimney. It is climbed in one pitch.

1. (30m) Ascend easy rock to the base of the chimney crack. This is climbed using a combination of the crack itself (good small/medium nut

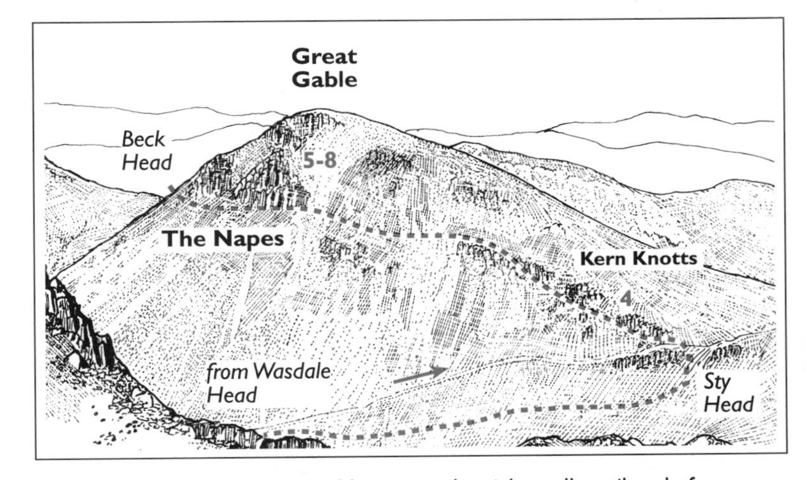

runners), and foot and handholds out on the right wall, until a platform is reached. Above this is a wide vertical crack, which can be climbed direct, or via the more open rib on its right hand side. This leads to a big ledge with small chockstone belay, backed up with nuts.

Most parties will wish to keep the rope on whilst scrambling up a further 20m or so, to grassy ledges above.

Next: from here, an easy descent (10 minutes) can be made to the right (facing out), either back to sacks, or directly to the path, to continue the journey to the Napes.

Napes Crags

On the Napes there are several good, and popular, routes graded Diff or V. Diff - Needle Ridge, in particular, can get very busy. For a fine day's mountaineering, it is recommended that the last route of the day should be climbed with sacks, allowing the trip to the summit of Great Gable to be made before returning to the valley.

Of the routes described, Needle Ridge is the first encountered if approaching from Sty Head and Kern Knotts, and Arrowhead Ridge if approaching from Honister or directly from Wasdale Head by Gavel Neese.

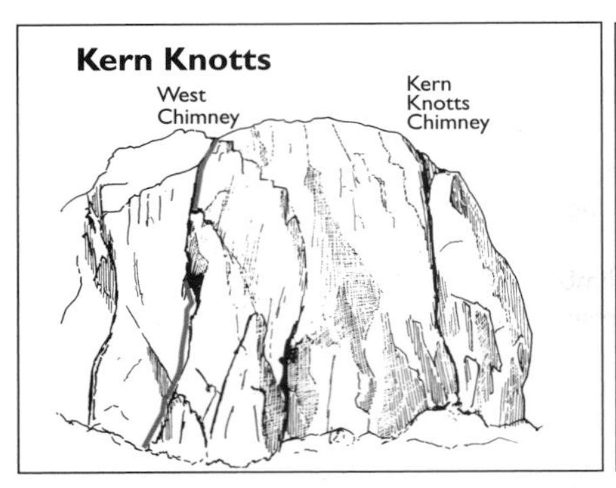

On the approach from Kern Knotts, the first big area of crag encountered is Tophet Wall. Although this day out does not include a route in this steep and intimidating area, it is worth noting as the main descent route passes underneath it.

The scrambly path eventually leads into the scree filled Napes Gully, with Napes Needle rising above this on its right-hand side. Go up the gully until almost level with the base of the Needle and follow polished rocks leading leftwards out of the gully, to reach an area known as the Dress Circle, which provides entertaining views of the antics on the Needle. This is the starting place for Abbey Buttress and Eagle's Nest Ordinary.

If the path is followed further round left, a second gully is crossed. The ridge on the far side of this gully is Arrowhead Ridge, which can be identified by the 'arrowhead' or prominent diamond-shaped pinnacle which forms its apex, above which it continues upwards at a more gentle angle for the rest of its length.

Descent (or onward) routes are the same for all four routes, and are detailed after Route 8.

5. Needle Ridge 100m V. Diff initially, rapidly giving way to Diff

Guide Time 1 1/2 hours

An excellent route, and one of the most popular in the area. If you don't like crowds, get here early, and avoid sunny weekends! The rock is now highly polished, which makes route-finding easy. As the climb is clean, sound and well-protected, the polished holds don't add to the difficulty except on the starting moves. Most of the route was first climbed in 1884 by Haskett-Smith. The direct (now the normal) start was added in 1911.

Start from the gap immediately behind the Needle. The pitches described are traditionally short, and may be run together.

1. (12m) The initial slab is climbed by delicate, very polished holds, which succumb to a positive approach. Continue up a leftwards slanting deep groove. Above this a stance may be taken below a steep wall.

2. (15m) Climb the steep wall above, followed by easier rocks, and climb a second wall. Traverse rightwards to a rib to belay.

3. (25m) Climb the rib into a corner, ascending this on its right to belay below a wall with a prominent groove to its left.

4. (12m) Climb the groove, either direct or by using a combination of holds on its right wall.

5. (35m) Easy scrambling leads to the top.

6. Eagle's Nest Ordinary 110m Diff

Guide time about 1 1/2 hours

With a good selection of chimneys, this is definitely an outing in the traditional style! First climbed in 1892.

Start: the route will climb the obvious wide chimney at the left end of the Dress Circle, which is a good place to leave sacks.

1. (30m) Scramble to the bottom of the chimney, which, when dry, is easier than it looks. Some bridging is required but there are plenty of good holds (sometimes hidden!) Belay at the top of the chimney.

2. (12m) Climb up through the gap that is formed by a slab and a huge 'totem pole' pinnacle, both on the right-hand side of the stance. Continue up the slab to belay in a corner.

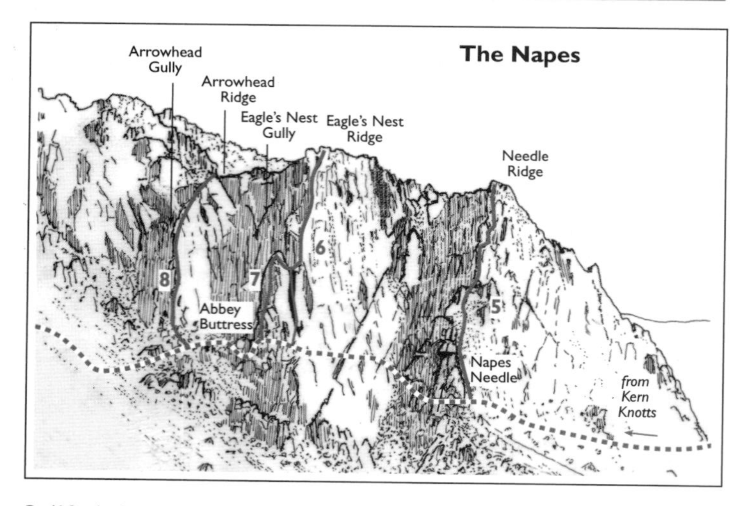

3. (12m) Climb the short but strenuous chimney above the corner until a ledge is reached. Resist the temptation to continue up the crack system: instead step onto the ridge to its left. Climb this by well-worn slabs to a ledge at the foot of a wall that's divided by short crack chimneys on either side. Here a convenient belay can be taken.

4. (18m) Either the polished crack on the left, or the less polished chimney on the right, may be taken to gain the top of the wall. Both are quite strenuous for the short! Follow easy broken rocks to the top of the final pinnacle.

5. (35m) Easy scrambling remains, to the col at the top of the Napes Buttresses.

7. Abbey Buttress 60m V. Diff

Guide time approximately 2 hours

This is a harder but cleaner alternative to Eagle's Nest Ordinary, offering exposed, well-protected climbing before eventually joining that previous route. First climbed in 1909.

Start: from the Dress Circle, continue left under the first pitch of Eagle's Nest Ordinary, until the path squeezes behind a huge detached flake. Abbey Buttress starts here.

1. (20m) Ascend the well worn wall above the path to a ledge. Step right, below a big pinnacle, and up a steep crack system to a commodious belay ledge.

2. (20m) This pitch looks intimidating, but with some devious route finding affords good climbing on positive holds. Go straight up the steep rock behind the belay, to a ledge at about 5m. Move left to the end of the ledge, and climb up for about 8m. From here a clean, polished traverse line leads rightwards, below a small overhang, to a rib. The rib is climbed on jugs to a huge, bouldery ledge.

3. (20m) Climb the crack on the left edge of the wall above. This leads you into a leaning corner - both crack and corner are much easier than they look. Above this, climb cracks and steps to a shared belay at the top of Pitch 3 on Eagle's Nest Ordinary. Complete as for that route.

8. Arrowhead Ridge Direct 80m V. Diff

Guide time 2 hours

Steep and exposed climbing, with an Alpine character. First climbed, in two stages, in 1892 and 1893.

Start: having identified Arrowhead Ridge as above, start at its lowest point.

1. (15m) Climb the easy rocks of the lower ridge, followed by a steeper section to a belay ledge.

2. (25m) The ridge steepens above. Climb straight up it to a small pinnacle. From its top step onto the slab on its right, then make an exposed and difficult rightward traverse under the overhang of the arrowhead to enter the notch behind it. Alternatively, pass the arrowhead on its left side - equally exposed but easier. Belay in the notch.

3. (10m) Climb steeply up the Wasdale face to the tip of the Arrowhead then make a wild step across the gap and climb up cracks to reach the horizontal crest of the ridge. Belay a few metres along this. Take care to protect the second on this pitch.

4. (30m) Scramble along the ridge.

Descent: eventually all the component ridges combine, and drop across a small col to run into the stony main mountainside of Great Gable. If doing another climb, drop into the huge red scree gully on the right, below the south east end of the ridge. It leads through a rocky narrowing to the Tophet Wall area. The easiest (and eponymous) route up this daunting wall is, perhaps surprisingly, 'only' Hard Severe: something to aspire to? It avoids the extremely steep headwall by traversing to the right. Due to the looseness of the scree, allow at least 30 minutes to return to your sacks.

And Now?

Any of the routes on the Napes, if climbed with rucksacks, will put you in a good position to proceed to the summit of Great Gable. A faint track leads from the neck of the ridge where the routes finish. This is followed upwards and leftwards to join a main walkers' path (very rocky - look for the cairns) southwest of the summit. More direct lines can be taken by careful scrambling straight up the crowning craglets. About 40 minutes to the top.

Most descents from Gable are steep and rocky. By far the most pleasing way off is to take the north-easterly track, leading down into Windy Gap. From this col, either descend via Aaron Slack to Sty Head Tarn for a return to Seathwaite, or continue over Green Gable for high level routes back to Honister (over Brandreth) or Seathwaite (over Base Brown). Route 25 (Gamma, Diff) can be incorporated into the ascent of Green Gable.

Kirkfell Expedition

Kirkfell is one of the less inspiring Lakeland hills – a steep lump with a plateau instead of a summit. This hidden scramble provides an ascent far more exciting than one would expect from such an apparently tame mountain. Ill Gill is a reminder that the fells are never dull, but reserve their wildness for those who make the effort to find it.

Approach from the Wasdale Head Inn, taking the footpath behind the pub along Lingmell Beck towards Great Gable. Immediately after the crossing of a long wooden footbridge, a path leads steeply up Gavel Neese; Gable Beck is just below this path on the left. Head to the first bump on the path.

Ill Gill is now obvious as a gorse-edged ravine reaching almost to the top of Kirkfell. There are no other features on this flank of the hill. From the path bump, a short thrash through the bracken brings you to the foot of the gill.

9. Ill Gill Grade 3 with short sections of Diff

Vertical Height around 350m: guide time about 2 1/2 hours hours for a semi-roped ascent

Most of the route is straightforward, but steep walls and gorse thickets enclose the lower reaches of the gill, barring safe and easy exit. This, and the presence of much friable rock, make the expedition a serious undertaking. There are a few sections where short but awkward moves constitute actual rock climbing of Diff standard and where failure would result in a nasty fall. It is recommended that a rope be used to protect these sections, particularly in damp conditions. Due to the danger of its dragging over loose rock, however, it is not recommended to rope the other, easier, sections.

It's in the abundance of pools and cascades that the attraction of this route lies. However, normal water levels or greasy conditions would make it too serious a proposition to be enjoyable. Choose a prolonged dry period for the ascent, preferably on a sunny day.

Start at the point where Ill Gill flows into Gable Beck at a pretty pool. Enter the gill and scramble over easy-angled rocks past pools to a 12m high waterfall. Bypass this by the wall on its right. The move to get established on the wall is difficult, and leads to big but slimy holds. Scramble easily on until another small cascade provides an awkward problem, which succumbs to strenuous determination.

A long, unclimbable cascade now lies ahead; so, just above the awkward problem, look out for the escape route up the right-hand wall.

(You can scramble on up to the cascade for a better look, but you will have to return to this point.) The wall to be escaped up is steep and vegetated, but the way has been gardened and is obvious.

Walk up the hillside close to the edge of the ravine for a few minutes, until above the waterfall. Re-enter the gill down a rocky rib. At the foot of the rib, tall people can drop down a short quartz wall into the gill bed, while shorties will need to clatter down a metre or two of the scree.

The scrambling is easy again for a while, climbing a number of attractive cascades to reach one that flows down a slabby wall. This is climbed on its left on juggy holds. At the top a second cascade blocks the way. This is climbed on its right-hand side. The first 3m of this are steep and awkward, on rounded holds which look more positive than they are, giving some excitement. Move left around a rib to easier ground.

The next waterfall runs down a very steep wall. It is doubtful if this is climbable even in dry conditions except as a severe rock pitch. The only solution, therefore, is to by-pass the fall by a gardened escape on the vegetated wall immediately to its left. This is loose, but the angle isn't too steep, and with care it is fairly straightforward.

Above is an amphitheatre with a stepped cascade at its back flowing into a round pool. Favourable conditions for a direct ascent are unlikely, so escape via some big rock holds and steep heather on the right-hand edge of the amphitheatre.

Return to the gill down easy grass slopes into a very open section of the gill bed, where it is floored with large scree boulders. Climb easily to a junction where a tiny tributary enters from the right above a small scree shoot.

Follow the main (left-hand) watercourse up a cascade and over more large scree. This leads to pleasant climbing up the right side of a cascade marked with patches of pink rock.

Where the stream enters the ravine over a steep wall on the left, exit via a rib to the left of the watercourse to finish the route. The beck still flows above, but gives no more scrambling and should now be abandoned in order to make your way to the summit.

And Now?

About 20 minutes of steep rough walking up grass and rock will bring you to Kirkfell Tarn, on the summit plateau. Turn left (southwest) to reach the summit cairn in about five minutes. From here there is a choice of three descents back to Wasdale Head. The quickest is by an initially well-cairned but otherwise vague track southwest from the summit, which drops steeply and directly towards the pub, via Highnose Head. It involves some badly eroded scree and is not kind on the knees. However, it will get you to a pint of nerve-restoring Gable Bitter in about one hour.

The alternatives are longer but pleasanter. Leave the summit by the path to the northwest, dropping down a rather rocky rib to Black Sail Pass to follow a good path down by Mosedale Beck and Ritson's Force. Or retrace your steps past Kirkfell Tarn to Beck Head Tarn – either of these descents will take between 1 1/2 and 2 hours.

Pillar Expedition

300m scrambling, 205m climbing: up to V. Diff (including Low Man)
OR 200m scrambling, 140m climbing: up to Diff (excluding Low Man)

Pillar Rock, rising from the northeast flank of Pillar mountain, is one of the most impressive crags in Lakeland. It has many high-quality climbs covering most of the grading spectrum, though the upper 'E' grades are under-represented.

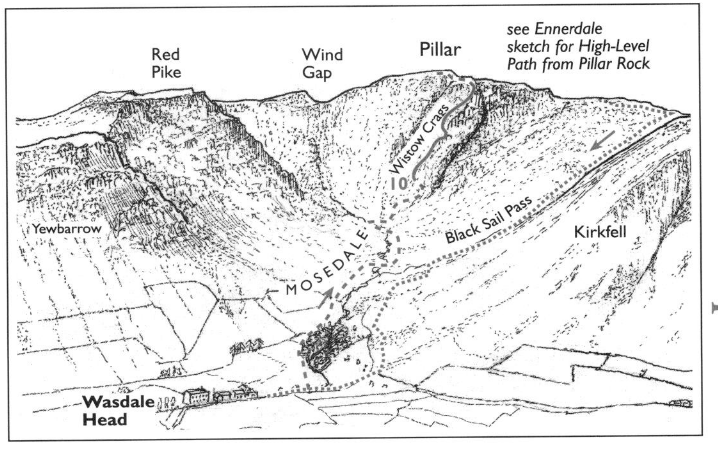

As the climbs end on the rock's own summits, High Man or Low Man, they don't usually involve a visit to the summit of Pillar mountain itself. However, the itinerary described here combines a pleasant scramble on the southwest side of Pillar mountain, a visit to the top, and then a descent to the Rock itself. The suggested full-on expedition then climbs over all three summits of the Rock, adding up to a challenge of truly Alpine proportions. The shorter version is still no mean day out, climbing to High Man by one of the finest routes - of any grade - in the western Lakes.

10. Wistow Crags Grade 2

Vertical Height 200m: guide time about one hour.

A fairly straightforward outing, though difficulties can be sought out for added sporting interest. It is infinitely preferable to the miserable screes of Wind Gap.

Approach

From Wasdale Head cross the old pack-horse bridge and go up on the left hand side of the valley, with the stream on your right. Near the head of the valley are a number of boulders including the 'Y' Boulder - grid ref 178104, named on some OS maps. These were much loved by the early climbers for an additional diversion - but where did they find the time? We surely can't dally... Another path angles across from the other side of the valley to meet our route and then climb towards the scree-run/path up to Wind Gap that scars the head of the valley.

Three rocky sections rise above the valley on the southern flank of Pillar. On closer viewing the first of these (Murl Rigg) becomes a vague jumble, and the furthest away becomes foreshortened, leaving Wistow Crags in the middle as two-tier sweep of clean rock, bounded by a gully on its left hand side. Strike up the fellside to the foot of the first section. Approximately 1 1/2 hours from Wasdale Head.

Start at the lowest point of the crag at a sort of grassy platform. Climb a series of clean ribs, generally working leftwards, to reach the top of the first tier. At the foot of the second tier, ascend a broad rib. Walk left along the ledge above to climb slabs on the left edge of the buttress. Easy-angled scrambling then leads to the neck of the buttress. Walk up grassy slopes towards the rocky ribs rising above the left-hand gully. Climb either side of a sharp, prominent flake, and once above it, keep to the right-hand side of the upper buttress, until the scrambling runs out within easy striking distance of the path along the summit ridge.

Next: Turn left (northwest) up this path to reach the summit shelter and trig point in about 20 minutes. From another large cairn at the northern edge of the summit plateau the top of Pillar Rock is visible below. A small path starts down the steep Ennerdale face, then contours 100m right, to the crest of a small spur, immediately above the Rock. The main summit is High Man. In front of it lies a lower rock-summit, known as Pisgah. Descend to the col in front of Pisgah by the well-worn, eroded path, or scrambling alongside it.

Pillar Rock

The area around Pillar Rock is very complex, with several approaches and descents in addition to the ones described here: all of them demand care and good route-finding. It is sensible to study our diagrams and

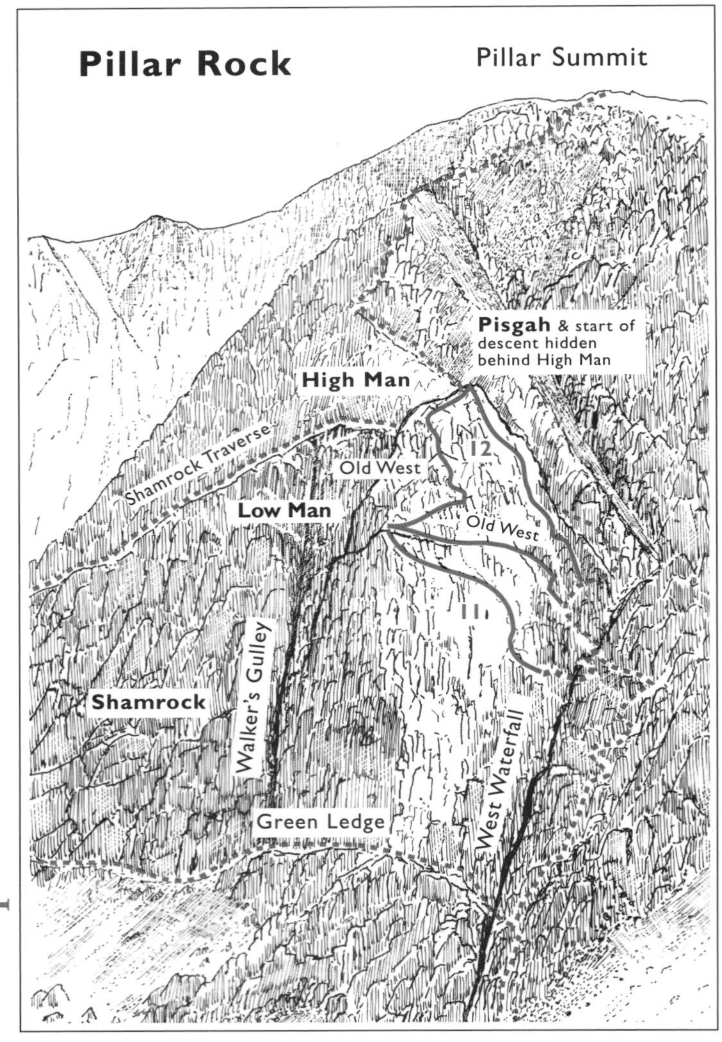
Pillar Rock
Pillar Summit
Pisgah & start of descent hidden behind High Man
High Man
Shamrock Traverse
12
Old West
Low Man
Old West
11
Shamrock
Walker's Gulley
West Waterfall
Green Ledge

information in advance of your outing to familiarise yourself with the general layout and features. Those wishing to reach the climbs on Pillar Rock from Wasdale without the preliminary scramble on Wistow Crags can do so by the High-level Path: that approach is described at the end of the climbing routes on the Rock. Those wishing to get to Pillar Rock from Ennerdale can also use the High-level Path from Black Sail. For them there is also a more direct route by way of the West Waterfall, but we shall not describe that here.

Approach to Routes 11 and 12 (West Face of Pillar Rock)

Sacks may be left in the col directly before Pisgah, before descending to the left (west) on a climbers' path which drops down into a wide scree-filled gully. This descends below the west face of Pisgah, and past the obvious gap of West Jordan Gully, which separates Pisgah from High Man's soaring west face.

A little further down, there is a large rock embedded in the gully bed. About 15m below this is the start of the New West (Route 12); just below and to the left again is the start of an obvious diagonal break which separates High Man and Low Man; this is the Old West Route, by which the first ascent of the Rock was made in 1826. But if the full expedition is to be undertaken, continue down the wide scree-filled gully to the point where it very obviously stops being wide and scree-filled and drops away dramatically into a steep sided, cascade-washed chasm. This is the West Waterfall. Great care must be taken in crossing above the top of the Waterfall to avoid dislodging stones (or yourself!) down into it: the climbers' access route from Ennerdale involves a tricky traverse across the waterfall's foot.

11. West Wall Climb 65m V. Diff

Guide time 1 hour 15 minutes

A good way for rock-gluttons to make a complete ascent, this route wanders pleasantly through the territory of much harder climbs, with nicely contrasting pitches. A faint polish betrays its long-ago popularity. Though clean and sound, the route feels left behind by time. If you were to meet another party on the route, you wouldn't be surprised to see them attired in tweeds and nailed boots, like the first ascent party in 1919.

Start: From the top of the West Waterfall, cross ledges to a small, square, grassy platform, about 12m above the level of the top of the waterfall, below a short (3m) wall with a prominent broken crack.

1. (15m) Climb the broken crack and make an easy semi-mantleshelf move onto a grass ledge. Climb a V-shaped chimney-groove, then up steep rocks to a sloping ledge with a good flake belay near its left end.

2. (15m) A short traverse right leads to a broad sloping rock shelf. Climb a crack in the wall on the right to reach a good ledge. Do not be tempted to climb the continuation of the crack, as this will take you off-route.

3. (15m) Make a leftward rising traverse to big blocks with good flake belays.

4. (20m) Step left and climb the short arete formed by the blocks, and then a steep and awkward groove that provides a genuine crux to the route. Easy climbing then leads to a grassy terrace just below the summit of Low Man.

Next: from the top of Low Man, walk down to the col before the steep northern face of High Man. If West Wall Climb took longer than planned, and there isn't time for New West, shed a tear and then head directly on up the Old West to High Man. If the original plan remains in place, descend the lower part of the Old West. It is probably wise as well as convenient to stay roped either way.

Old West Route: lower section: descent. Grade 2

Vertical height 40m: guide time 20 minutes

The Old West slants down on the right, a steep rock gangway with large and well-worn holds and considerable exposure. From its foot walk a few metres up the scree to the foot of the New West (Route 12).

Old West Route: upper section: ascent. Grade 3

Vertical height 50m, guide time 30 minutes.

The well-trodden way slants up left, then back right, to the foot of a steep and exposed little 3m chimney. This arrives onto High Man's flat summit.

12: New West Climb 87m Diff

Guide time about 1 1/2 hours, but this is a popular route in Pillar terms, so allow extra time if following other parties.

Glorious climbing on clean rock, still rough despite the polish of many years of popularity. Nowhere is this climb too exacting, with plentiful protection and comfortable stances, yet it enjoys a truly Alpine feel. First climbed in 1901 by a party including George and Ashley Abraham. Once the correct start has been established, route finding is easy – follow the clean rock between the well-worn and obvious stances.

Approach: whether direct from Pisgah, or via West Wall Climb and Old West, this has already been described.

Start about 15m below the large rock embedded in the gully, just above the foot of the Old West.

1. (20m) Begin easily up clean rock, trending a little to the left. Climb a rib and short corner, then follow steep steps with good holds to an accommodating ledge.

2. (10m) A wide crack (or is it a shallow chimney?) is climbed to a small platform. From here make a short (4m) traverse left to a belay.

3. (17m) Climb a groove, then make a leftwards traverse across slabs to the foot of a chimney. Thread belays.

4. (20m) The chimney can be climbed with relative elegance by using holds on its outside, or thrutched direct in a more traditional manner. Part way up, the way is barred by an obvious chockstone. Traverse rightwards just below it, climbing over a pile of blocks on the way, to reach a good belay.

5. (20m) Complete the climb by ascending the slab immediately above the stance, and finish on the summit of High Man.

And Now?

It is not unusual for successful summit teams to be totally flummoxed about how to get off the perpendicular top of High Man, across Jordan

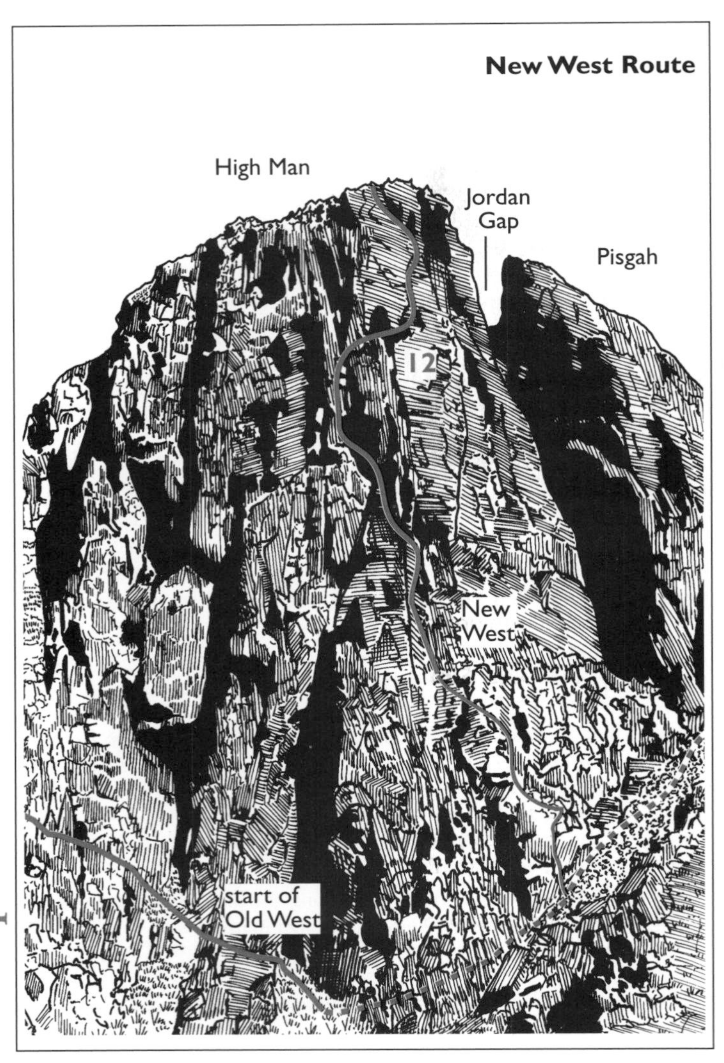
New West Route
High Man
Jordan
Gap
Pisgah
12
New
West
start of
Old West

Gap and up to Pisgah. (Some even resort to abseiling.) In fact, descent from High Man is via a fine route called Notch and Slab. When this route is done in ascent it is known as Slab and Notch, the features being encountered in reverse order.

13. Notch and Slab 50m Moderate

Guide time: 20 minutes

Start on the summit of High Man. Initial directions assume you are facing outwards as you descend. Walk down northwards (towards the High Stile ridge on the other side of Ennerdale) for about 10m, to locate a chimney on the right (east) side. Descend this, and follow polished holds to the right (i.e. towards Pillar Mountain) to gain a stepped slab. Descend this to a ledge.

Now the route description, and you, will be facing in towards the rock. Move left (i.e. towards Pillar Mountain) to a short arete and descend this to another ledge. Move left again to the Notch, go through it, and descend the corner beyond it. A final short step gains the eponymous Slab. Walk all the way along the foot of the slab to a crack, then climb down again to a ledge. This leads to the hillside near the foot of East Jordan Gully.

In good visibility this is much less complicated than it sounds as the way is well trodden, but if darkness is closing in, or in an emergency of any kind, it is possible to make that short abseil - about 16m - from the summit of High Man direct into Jordan Gap; you'll have to sacrifice a long sling. This eliminates the descent of Notch and Slab, and is therefore quicker, but altogether misses the point of a mountaineering day out.

One summit of the Rock remains: Pisgah. Ascend East Jordan Gully to the gap (Jordan Gap) between Pisgah and High Man. Turn towards Pisgah and climb it by holds on the right hand side: this looks far more intimidating than it actually is, but there is nothing to be lost by keeping the rope on. This brings you to the top of Pisgah in a few moves of Grade 3. From there, an easy (Grade 1) scramble, with mild exposure and good rock, leads down to the col between Pisgah and the main mountainside.

Descent by the High-level Path to Black Sail

The best descent for either Wasdale or Ennerdale is by the High-level Path to the Black Sail Pass. About 2 hours to Wasdale Head. From the sack-dump col below Pisgah, a path contours eastwards around the head

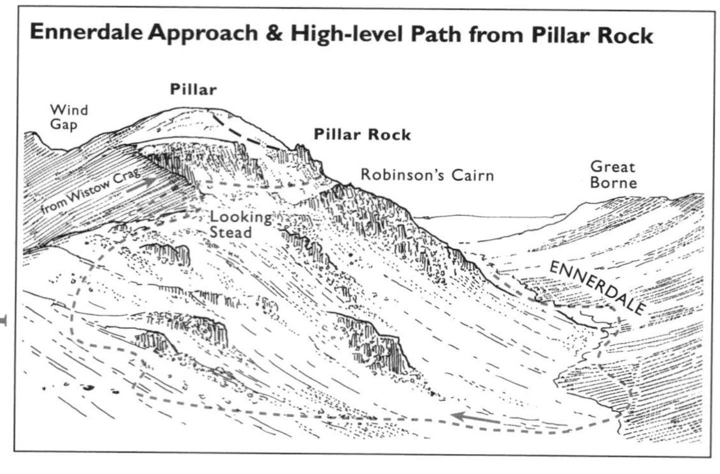

of a scree bowl called the Amphitheatre. Back across the Amphitheatre, and at the same level as the path, you look at the notch of Notch and Slab. Don't descend into the Amphitheatre: it runs down into Walker's Gully, so-called not because it's suitable for walkers but rather because the first person killed there happened to be a Mr Walker.

To the east of Pillar Rock, a large buttress leans against the face of Pillar Mountain. This is the Shamrock (so-called because it isn't Pillar Rock). The path descends a few metres, then slants down the top edge of the Shamrock on a rock shelf - this Shamrock Traverse is exposed, but does not involve any scrambling or climbing. Once across the top of the Shamrock, the path descends a short scree-run into Pillar Cove. At the lip of the cove on the right is the big Robinson's Cairn. From here a small path (or rather, two paths, one above the other) contour eastwards across the steep face of Pillar Mountain, to reach the mountain's east ridge at the foot of its steep section.

A ridge path leads on past the slight rise of Looking Stead, with a short-cut path down right into Mosedale (for Wasdale Head) or a continuation ahead to Black Sail Pass (for either Wasdale Head or Ennerdale).

Approach to Pillar Rock by the High-level Path

This is just the previous descent-route in reverse. Reach Black Sail Pass from Wasdale Head via Mosedale, or from Ennerdale. From the pass, head west along the gently rising ridge. The path skirts to left of Looking Stead, to the col between it and PIllar mountain. In another 100m it reaches a tiny, second col, then climbs much more steeply. 20m up this steeper rise is a neat little cairn. Here look round on the right to find the start of the High-level Path. This contours along the steep face above Ennerdale, to reach the large Robinson's Cairn. At this point there is a sudden and stunning view of Pillar Rock.

Cross the floor of Pillar Cove towards the Rock, then head uphill along a gentle rock rib. A steep little scree path runs up to left of Shamrock Buttress, then turns right, along its top, on the slanting ramp of the Shamrock Traverse. At the end of this you arrive at the rim of the scree-bowl called the Amphitheatre. Opposite, across the Amphitheatre, is the east face of High Man, and on its left the lower pinnacle of Pisgah. Contour around the top edge of the Amphitheatre to reach the col to left (south) of Pisgah, between it and the main mountainside. About 3 hours from Wasdale Head.

Steeple Expedition

Lying on the western side of the wonderfully named Mirk Cove, Steeple provides some of the remotest climbing in Lakeland. Although lacking the climbing quality of some of the routes described in this guide, the feeling of splendid isolation makes the long hike well worthwhile. The foot of the climb is a long uphill trek from either Ennerdale or Wasdale, with the Wasdale approach being slightly the less arduous of the two. The only public transport to Ennerdale is the Ennerdale Rambler free bus service, which links the main towns of West Cumbria with the car park at Bowness Knott. This runs on summer Sundays and Bank Holidays only, and gives you 5 1/2 hours to walk in, climb the route, and get back to Bowness Knott - very fit climbers in training for Alpine exploits may regard this as an ideal challenge.

Approach: from Ennerdale

From the Bowness Knott car park, follow a forest road along the side of the lake, until the beck can be crossed at the Irish bridge (grid ref 134142). Follow the main forestry track over another beck-crossing to a further footbridge (grid ref 151138). Just past this, a finger-post marked

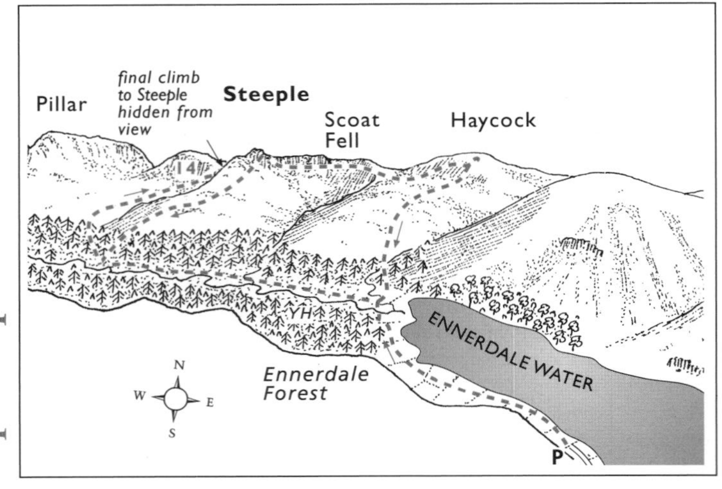

'Pillar' directs you to the right up the hill. Go up this rough path to another forestry track. Turn left along this until another sign marked 'Pillar' directs you up the fellside towards High Beck. Follow the faint path alongside High Beck into Windgap Cove. Steeple East Buttress is the obvious buttress which rises from the right-hand side of the upper cove (Mirk Cove) and goes straight to the summit of Steeple. About 2 1/2 hours on foot: this may be reduced by cycling as far as the first finger post.

Approach: from Wasdale Head
The shorter way is along Mosedale, past its waterfalls, eventually taking the left-hand path direct to the top of Wind Gap. The screes below Wind Gap are severely eroded and need to be climbed with extreme care and patience. Turn left along the ridge towards Little Scoat Fell, and drop down into Mirk Cove via some easy screes on its eastern side. From here it is a short walk across the cove to the foot of the buttress. Time 2 1/2 hours.

The horrors of Wind Gap can be avoided by a longer approach following the Overbeck path around the western side of Yewbarrow to Dore Head and onto Red Pike and Scoat Fell – about 3 hours.

14. Steeple East Buttress 155m V. Diff

Guide time 3 hours

The pleasure of the route lies in the way it starts at the bottom of the buttress and climbs over 150 metres directly to the summit – and apart from the silhouettes of walkers on the Scoat Fell ridge you will not see another soul. It's another measure of the route's remoteness that its first recorded ascent was not made until 1957.

From Mirk Cove it is useful to study the line of the route in advance. Easy scrambling over broken rocks will lead to the foot of the long clean buttress. This is followed to a definite break at about half height, where a grass rake slants up to the right. The route finishes by the sweep of rocks above and left of the rake, directly to the top.

Although the climbing offers few technical difficulties, some skill is required to find good runner placements and belays. The rock on the lower section is clean, rough and sound. After the grass break the rock is shattered and care must be exercised in the choice of holds and to avoid the rope's dislodging loose pieces onto the second.

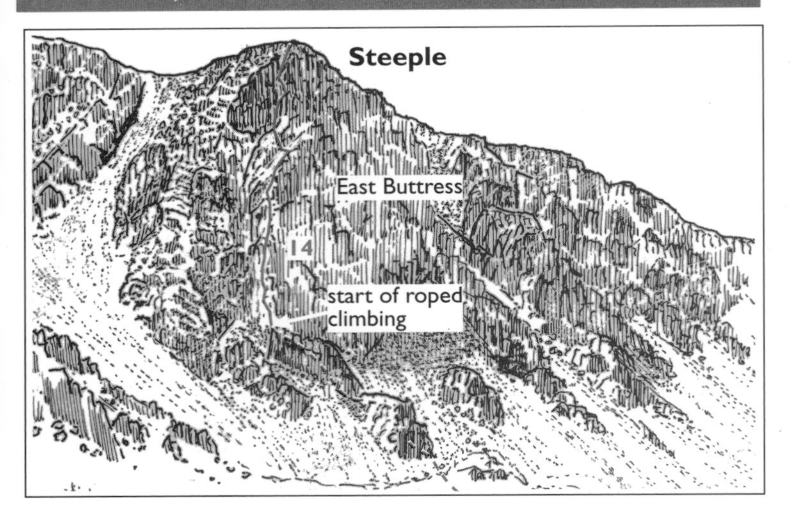

Start from the lowest point of the clean continuous rock, which forms a distinct ridge.

1. (30m) From the foot of the buttress, climb easily up the ridge to a good ledge at the foot of a short steep wall.

2. (15m) Climb the short wall to a grass ledge. The continuation wall is climbed by a fine crack on its right-hand side, which leads to a recess with thread belays.

3. (35m) Step left from the belay to regain the main ridge and follow this, with increasing steepness, until it eases just below the grassy rake. Belay on a good flake.

4. (20m) This section involves a careful walk up the grass rake, sprinkled with loose rock, moving up to the next section of the ridge, which rises on the left of the grass. Belay at the bottom of a wall of very jagged rock, bounded on its right by a crack.

5. (24m) Ascend the jagged wall and the stepped ridge above until a stance can be taken at the foot of dark and somewhat overhanging rocks just below the summit.

6. (30m) To the left of the stance there are two grooves, both rather dirty. Make a couple of moves towards the left-hand one, then climb directly up the rib that separates the two. From the top of the rib easy scrambling leads to the summit, where, if a 16-foot sling has been carried for the purpose, it is possible to belay from Steeple's actual summit block! Otherwise a normal 8-foot sling allows a comfortable belay to be taken just below.

And Now?

From the top of Steeple, you can descend into Ennerdale straight down the north ridge, re-entering the forest near the Low Beck waterfalls. For other descents walk along the narrow ridge to the main Scoat Fell ridge, from where you can head over Red Pike (with the option of a nerve-racking descent of Dorehead Screes) or extend your walk west over Haycock (down to Ennerdale via Tewit How, to Wasdale via Nether Beck). All options take around 1 1/2 hours.

Upper Eskdale Expedition

550m scrambling (plus long horizontal sections in Esk Gorge): up to Grade 3

In its upper reaches the Esk flows through one of the loveliest landscapes in Lakeland - starting in the high eyrie of Esk Hause, below the impressive walls of Esk Buttress, through the broad expanse of Great Moss, and finally down through the gorge with its blue pools and lively waterfalls. The day out suggested here links these various delights by working its way up the dale via three scrambles of very different character.

To include Esk Gorge in the trip, approach must be made from Brotherilkeld, which is the way described here. Parking is available in a couple of large grassy pull-offs near the foot of Hardknott Pass.

It is possible to use the 'Laal Ratty' train from Ravenglass to Dalegarth Station, near Boot. From here it is 3km to Brotherilkeld - a lovely walk if you use the paths east of the river. Time can be saved by cycling: it is possible to take bikes on the train, subject to space being available, at £2 per single journey.

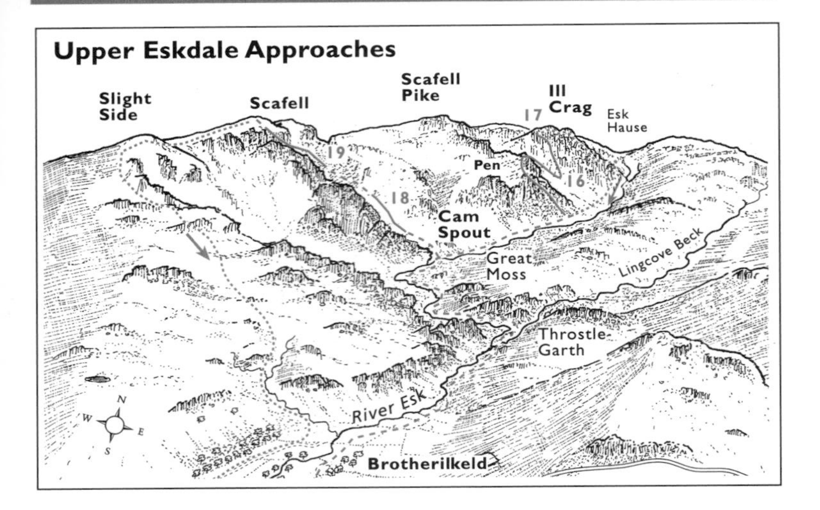

15. Esk Gorge Grade 2 although this can vary according to the state of the water.

Vertical Height – 150m over a horizontal distance of nearly a kilometre
Guide time 1 1/2 to 2 hours, but it is possible to break out at many places

Choose a dry period for optimum conditions. Except at exceptionally low water, you need to be prepared for a little paddling, as you wind your way through a world of rock walls and waterfalls hidden from the walkers sweating their way up the path above.

Approach: take the track behind the telephone box and follow the footpath that runs to left of Brotherilkeld Farm and then up-valley to right of the river to the confluence of Lingcove Beck and the Esk - about 45 minutes walk. A tiny packhorse bridge spans Lingcove Beck; the main path crosses this and continues up above the Esk (the stream on the left).

Start: Cross the bridge. Just above the confluence there is an impassable pool. Enter the Esk gorge just above this.
Initially the gorge has an open aspect, gradually becoming deeper and

more forbidding. Throughout this long trip, the best policy is to stick as close to the watercourse as possible, working out your own way via easy rocks, clean with good holds. The twists and turns of the river with its numerous pools and waterfalls sometimes give the impression that there is no way through. Scan the options from various angles, criss-crossing the stream via frequent boulders and ridges of rock. At low water, an easy way through will be found, usually following the cleanest rock.

High up in the ravine and well into the trip, the most serious section is encountered with a traverse of the right wall, just above a deep pool. This looks impossible, and certain to result in a dunking, but is passable with care. From here cross slabs to where a huge boulder blocks the ravine. Climb the crack on its right hand side. Once into the easy, open section above the journey is almost over, and escape can be made onto the paths above (there are footpaths on both banks).

To prolong the expedition, continue to the final waterfall. This is much harder than anything else encountered, and path is invitingly close, so that this final assault is tackled more often than completed!

Next: You emerge below Scar Lathing Crag. The walkers' path tracks left below this and then curls round into the wide open spaces of the Great Moss. Beyond this is the wall of the Scafell range, festooned with crags. The nearest is the vast, shaggy bulk of Cam Spout Crag. Further right, at about the same level, is the clean pyramid of Esk Buttress: head for this. Note that older OS maps call it Dow Crag; some also name Central Pillar, its most famous climb (a soft touch at E2).

16. Thor's Buttress and Pen Grade 3

Vertical Height 100m: guide time 30 minutes to an hour, if climbed unroped.

A steep but fairly straightforward scramble on clean rock, rapidly gaining the small summit of Pen below the rocky ramparts of Scafell Pike.

Approach: cross Great Moss by the driest way you can find, heading towards Esk Buttress. Traverse under the crag low down, to avoid the screes, until the ridges and buttresses to the far right of the crag become visible. An obvious cleft slashes virtually the full height of the

right-most buttress, deepening to a cave near the top. This is Thor's Cave, and its direct ascent involves a short Severe climb. Our route lies up the ridge to the left of the cleft.

Start at the foot of the ridge. The initial rocks are mossy, but scramble up them to reach a break to left of Thor's Cave. Above is a corner-crack, with some overhanging flakes to its left. Go left and then back right up a ramp that leads into a gully alongside the flakes. Go up this then exit on the left, behind the highest flake. Move left along a ledge and at its end climb steeply and pull up onto the top of a block.

The easier section above is best climbed on its right side, overlooking a gully (the continuation of the Thor's Cave cleft) to reach a steep, smooth, slabby area. Go left below a boulder, to reach a vegetated ledge, and follow this a few metres further left. Climb a scoop in easier-angled rock, on encouraging holds, then trend right until once again poised above the gully. An attractive rib is followed until it disappears into the grassy hillside.

Above and to the right is the distinct summit cone of Pen. Walk up towards this, eventually bearing slightly left to the lowest point of the rocks. From here tackle a series of grooves, working your way up clean rock and good holds to the top.

Next: Directly in front and higher are the lower ramparts of Scafell Pike. These could be scrambled at the same grade, to gain, after a further long walk, the summit of the Pike. However, not far to the north lies one of the longest scrambles in the district.
The summit of Pen is a good place to look across Little Narrowcove and study the flanks of Ill Crags to identify the next route.

17. Ill Crags, South East Face Grade 3

Vertical Height: 300m. Guide time 1 - 1 1/2 hours for an unroped ascent. Use of a rope on the crucial sections (the central slabs and the exposed buttresses above) will double this time.

Despite initial appearances, the rock on this face is almost continuous from the lower flanks to the summit. It gives a true mountaineering expedition, high above the valley bottom, on steep rough rock. The route is long, exposed, and potentially serious, and requires confident route-finding. A rope is advised.

There are many alternatives and a detailed route description for an ascent of this length through such complex terrain would be more confusing than helpful. This is a place for experienced scramblers with an exploratory spirit. The slight signs of previous traffic can provide some guidance. Look around for the cleanest rock. That rock is, on the whole, sound and there is an abundance of holds, but many moves are irreversible.

It is best to locate the start of the route from the vantage point of Pen, and to make sure that you still able to recognise this as you get nearer.

Start at a sweep of steep, narrow slabs, low down on the mid to right-hand section of the face that overlooks Little Narrowcove.

Climb clean slabs and buttresses, which show some signs of previous passage, to reach a grass terrace below the imposing sweep of the central slabs. With the protection of a rope and a few nuts and slings (or a cool nerve), you could ascend directly up the steep slabby walls. Easier routes lie to the right of these walls, working back to the left. Pick a line to connect short walls, ribs and flakes to gain the second main, grassy section.

Above this is a series of buttresses, divided by short gullies. Chose a buttress - any of them will involve easy though exposed rock climbing. Above the buttresses make a short walk rightwards over mixed grass, rock and screes to a clean rock rib. This is a pleasant staircase leading up to some broken boulders. Scramble over these to the summit of Ill Crags.

And Now?

The most straightforward way back to Brotherilkeld is by way of Esk Hause. From here, a descent of upper Eskdale is the most obvious and easiest route but covers much ground that has already been trodden earlier in the day. It does not take very much more effort to walk up to Esk Pike and then down its long, little-trodden and magnificently wild south ridge, bearing slightly left before Low Gait Crags to cross Lingcove Beck at about grid ref 236044. From here follow the beck down to rejoin the Esk and the outward route.

Scafell via Upper Eskdale Expedition

300m scrambling: up to Grade 3

Upper Eskdale also provides an unfrequented approach to the summit of Scafell. Linking the routes described with the descent via Slight Side makes a day in which the briefly encountered summit hordes will throw the loneliness of every other step into stark contrast.

Arrive at Great Moss from either Cockley Beck or Brotherilkeld as on the preceding expedition - with scrambling on the way in Esk Gorge (Route 16) if desired. From Brotherilkeld allow about 1 1/2 to 2 hours to the foot of the waterfall.

18. Cam Spout Grade 3

Vertical Height 100m: guide time about 30 minutes for an unroped ascent in conditions of low water.

Cam Spout is the obvious, near vertical waterfall which cascades down the fellside in two major falls. It is located to the right of Cam Spout Crag (the crag, but not the waterfall, is named on OS maps). The normal walkers' route to Mickledore goes up immediately to right of the cascade, and there are several places where escape can be made onto the path, but we will ignore this as far as possible. The aim is always to keep close to the water.

There is one section that is very serious when the water level is high. This can easily be avoided but the route is then much less interesting. Start at the pool below the first waterfall.

The route begins with a tricky traverse on the right side of this first pool. Then climb the wall to right of the waterfall on very good rock. From the bed of the second pool, once again ascend the right wall and follow the easy ridge above. This merges with the path to reach a big pool and cascade above.

This is the crux of the scramble and should not be attempted if there is too much water. The way lies on the left hand side of the fall, up mossy and slimy rocks. The holds are, however, quite positive, and the moss has been worn away from the crucial ones. At a steepening, an obvious line crosses to the right hand side of the stream, to the security of clean rock with very good holds. If the first section is too wet and slippery, it is easy to use the path to reach the second, right-hand section.
From here return to the watercourse as it flows through a sort of trench, and continue around pools and small falls. The scrambling is much easier now, but always attractive and interesting. A final cascade

blocks your way and may be tackled by a steep slab on the right hand side, leading to good holds.

Next: Exit into the combe dominated by the pyramid of Scafell.

19. Scafell South East Side Grade 3

Vertical Height 200m: guide time about 45 minutes to the Scafell ridge.

From the top of Cam Spout waterfalls, join the path for a short way. The head of the combe gives the appearance of an almost unbroken sweep of rock. This appearance is deceptive, with the route requiring some walking to link the two main sections of climbing.

Start: five minutes walk off the path brings you to the lowest rocks. Their right side has a sharply overhanging base. Left of the overhangs is a swathe of mossy slabs, but left again is a much cleaner ribbon of slab. Start at its base, the lowest point of the rocks.

Climb the clean slabs then make your way without undue difficulty up slabs and ribs above, to their top.

Walk to the much bigger sweep of slabs above and to the right. These are dominated by an overhang part-way up. Get onto the slabs via clean rocks on their left edge, and go up them into a groove system which runs up towards the overhang. Climb the grooves to an overhung recess 15m below the prominent overhang, then move back left towards the edge of the buttress. Follow this edge until it peters out into the hillside, then move back right to climb the front of the buttress. The buttress gradually breaks up into a jumble of disconnected ridges. Link these at will, for some pleasant scrambling that leads towards the steep final buttress.

Walk to the foot of the buttress, which gives the impression that it will yield only to serious rock climbing. To the right of the steep wall, a gangway slants leftwards. Follow this with care, until upwards progress is blocked by steep cracked walls. Avoid this serious terrain by making a short exposed move left onto easy rocks on the left of the face.

A little easy scrambling remains, followed by about 10 to 15 minutes of walking to reach the summit of Scafell.

And Now?

The easiest way back into Eskdale is by the path down to Foxes Tarn, to rejoin the main path from Mickledore. A finer return to Brotherilkeld can be made over Long Green and Slight Side, wild and unfrequented country where you are unlikely to meet anyone until you regain the valley floor at Taw House, where a footbridge leads across to Brotherilkeld

Broad Stand

Borrowdale & Buttermere

The climbing in Borrowdale is very accessible. This fact, the main reason for its present popularity, paradoxically meant that route development took place much later than in other valleys. For the early pioneers rock climbing was a way of practising for the Alps, therefore it was the high mountain crags leading to major summits that inspired them.

There was a flurry of activity in Borrowdale in the 1880s led by the famous Abraham Brothers who had a photographic shop in Keswick (now George Fisher's, the equally famous climbing shop). But Bentley

Beetham, who made his first forays onto the Borrowdale crags in 1921, started their intensive development. Even so it was 1946 before he turned his attention to Shepherd's Crag, now the hub of climbing in Borrowdale.

Access

All the Borrowdale crags are accessible by car, but parking is limited. Late arrivals can face severe (if not Very Severe) frustration, and then an unscheduled extra walk. Consider, instead, the excellent Borrowdale Rambler bus service (no. 79) from Keswick, which drops off at all key access points. Crucially, and unlike many other valley bus services, it runs into the evening, with the last bus back from Seatoller being after 6pm on Sundays and after 9pm on other days. If only they were all like this... And for a truly romantic arrival, the Derwentwater Launch from Keswick calls in at the jetty opposite the Swiss Lodore Hotel.

Other buses passing through Borrowdale are actually Honister Ramblers (77 or 77a) which make a circuit over Honister Hause and down the Buttermere Valley (or in the opposite direction.) These allow a day starting on the west side of the valley (Routes 21 - 25) to finish in

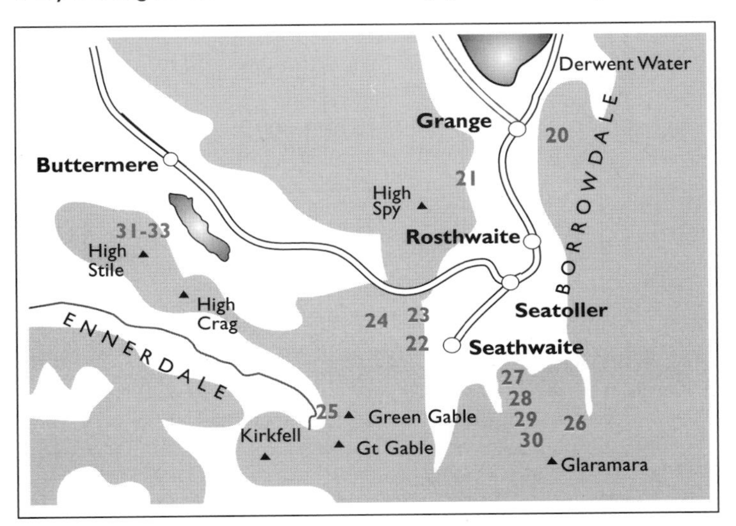

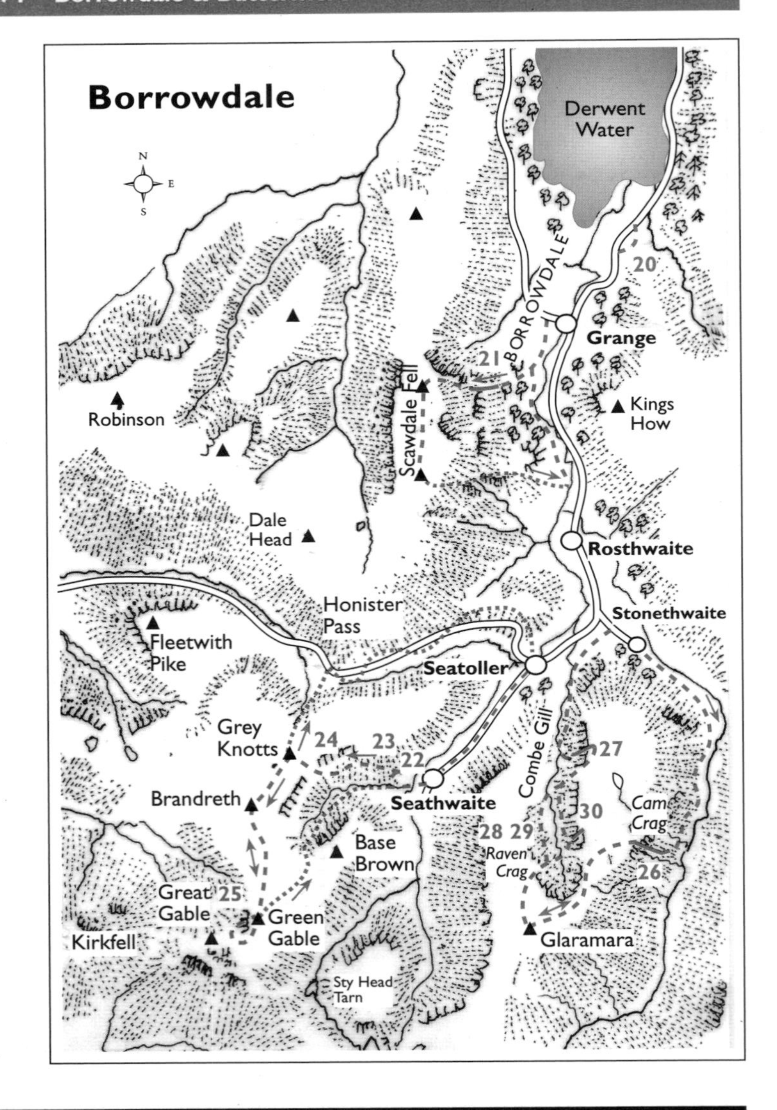
Borrowdale
N
E
S
Derwent Water
BORROWDALE
BORROWDALE
20
Grange
21
Kings How
Robinson
Scawdale Fell
Dale Head
Rosthwaite
Honister Pass
Stonethwaite
Fleetwith Pike
Seatoller
Grey Knotts
24
23
22
Combe Gill
27
Brandreth
Seathwaite
30
Cam Crag
28 29
Raven Crag
Base Brown
26
Great Gable
25
Green Gable
Kirkfell
Glaramara
Sty Head Tarn

the Fish at Buttermere village. Other Buttermere buses, and places to stay, are detailed before Route 31.

Amenities

Keswick makes a good base with a wide range of accommodation including a youth hostel, and a huge selection of cafes, pubs, restaurants and gear shops. There is even a cinema and theatre for entertainment on wet days, while your sleeping bag is drying in the launderette.

For a quieter base, camping options exist further up the valley with sites at Hollows Farm near Grange, one at Stonethwaite and another just south of Rosthwaite. Throughout the valley there are numerous hotels, B&Bs and self-catering cottages, ranging from the camping barn at Dinah Hoggus Rosthwaite and the two youth hostels to the swanky Swiss Lodore Hilton, which is handy for Shepherd's Crag, but probably not the right setting for tatty crag rats!

In the valley, the watering hole favoured by climbers is the public bar of the Scafell Hotel. Grange has a good selection of tea shops, but no climbing experience in Borrowdale is complete without a visit to the Shepherd's Crag Café, where large portions of home made cake are served with endless supplies of tea at slate tables in a barn. This is the place to hang out in your gear and catch the gossip about who has done what in the local climbing world.

There are a number of low-lying crags with routes of reasonable grade, including Quayfoot Buttress, Woden's Face and Bowderstone Crags - all accessible from the National Trust's Bowderstone car park, which actually lies directly below Quayfoot Buttress. However there is no question about the pre-eminent valley crag:

Valley Crag: Shepherd's Crag

For some crag rats, Shepherd's is the best crag in the Lakes - and not just because it's the shortest walk from the road, and has a really good café at the bottom. It's liable to be busy at pretty well any time of the day, week or year, and your climbing calls will all too often be obliterated by the traffic noise. That said, there are some excellent routes here, especially when it's cold and damp on the high fells, or when daylight is short. Mind you, there are some prominent climbers who boast of never

climber on the top pitch of Little Chamonix

having climbed here!

Where trees lie close to the rock they hold the moisture in, making for greasy conditions. However, the more open areas do dry fairly quickly. The absolute classic of the crag is Little Chamonix, which fortunately lies in one such area.

The crag is on the Borrowdale road, between the Swiss Lodore and Borrowdale Hotels. The Borrowdale Rambler bus will drop you at either. Alternatively it's just a short walk from the launch jetty opposite the Swiss Lodore Hotel.

There is limited free parking at High Lodore Farm, where the café is - if using this please park carefully so as to maximise space for others. If this is full, the best bet is to park at the National Trust car park at Kettlewell – a longer walk, but an attractive one along woodland paths. It is perfectly feasible to walk the 5km from Keswick, either along reasonable paths by the side of the road or, more attractively, along the lake shore, but this does rather negate the advantages of it being a roadside crag! However, to include a visit to the crag in a complete circuit of Derwentwater would certainly set you apart from the rest of the climbers there.

Approach: To reach the classic V. Diff of the crag it is easier to approach Shepherd's Crag from the Borrowdale Hotel (south) end. Take the path behind High Lodore Farm and over a stile. About 10m after the stile is a pleasant Diff called Jackdaw Ridge. Keep along the path, which is very distinct even as it crosses the boulder-strewn slope below a large wooded bay. Then the edge of the crag projects again. Little Chamonix starts here.

If approaching from the Swiss Lodore/Kettlewell direction (north of the crag), access is by an earthy path up through the trees. This became well worn during the Foot and Mouth outbreak in 2001, when it was the only access, but may fall back into disuse. It is handy if you are aiming for the Diffs and V. Diffs of Brown Slab, which is reached after about 5 minutes along this path. It is the big, easy angled slab at right angles to the main line of the crag – usually festooned with large parties of beginners. If you find it quiet, the routes are worth doing – single pitch, with easy route finding up the lines of polish. Avoid the corner though – this is a slippery VS.

From Brown Slabs direction, continue along the base of the crag, which becomes very broken and wooded before passing below an area of steep clean rock. There are some classic Severes and VS's here. From here cross open scree, rising slightly and then descending a little to the toe of the next buttress. Little Chamonix is just beyond the lowest point. This approach will take about 10-15 minutes from leaving the road.

Large numbers of climbers on, or waiting at the foot of, the route may confirm your location. If in any doubt, follow the track northwards for a few metres, to where it dips down to a wide rock bay with a large tree in it. The wall of the bay is split by a sharp-edged polished crack, which is Kransic Crack, a popular VS.

Having made a positive ID of Kransic Crack move up and right along the base of the crag until you locate a large pinnacle with a chimney-crack behind it. This is the start of the Mild Severe, Crescendo.

20. Little Chamonix 70m V. Diff

Guide time about 1 hour – but queues are likely at peak times
A couple of smaller nuts are useful

First ascent (solo) 26th May 1946 by Bentley Beetham. Since then the route has become legendary: well-known local climber Ray McHaffie has

made several ascents wearing boxing gloves and roller skates! But don't let such antics reduce your respect for it. The crux requires cunning and the exhilarating top pitch is very steep.

Start about 3m right of the Crescendo pinnacle, at a crack on the left side of some blocks.

1. (30m) Climb the well-polished crack. After about 10m move right into a leftwards-slanting groove. This is followed to a flake crack on the left, which quickly leads to excellent tree belays at the bottom of a wooded bay.

2. (12m) Scramble up between the trees towards two very obvious V-shaped corners. Belay below the left hand one.

3. (14m) This is the crux and has been known to delay progress for some time! Climb the left-hand corner to a prominent overhang. From here access is gained to a slab on the right by various means. The most professional way is to get onto the block immediately under the overhang and, from a scrunched position on its right edge, make a balancy stretch to holds on the slab. These are small and polished but perfectly adequate once you're established on them (though maybe not in boxing gloves and roller skates!). Climb the right edge of the slab to belay on the saddle at its top. Small nuts are useful for the belay, allowing you to stop where you can see your second and shout useful advice or derisive comments, whichever will be the most effective.

4. (14m) A spectacular and much photographed pitch. From the belay climb up and slightly right towards a pinnacle and step right just below it. The wall is slightly overhanging (to the nervous it may feel not so slightly!) but fabulous holds allow it to be climbed directly to an abrupt finish on a level terrace.

Descent from this part of the crag is quite tricky. Go to the right hand end of the terrace (facing uphill), where it disappears down a steep corner. Climb down the short, steep slab to the right (facing out) of the corner, using small, well-polished holds. Once this difficulty is passed the way is a straightforward descent through the trees back to the main path and rucksacks.

Gate Gill Crag Day

The River Derwent meanders from its source through leafy glades that provide pleasant easy walks along its course. This ambience is shared, but with more adventure and fewer people, by the scramble up one of its minor tributaries, Gate Gill. Not named on the OS maps, this is the gill that runs between Goat (or Gate) Crag and Nitting Haws, and is easily located from the Goat Crag path. The scrambling starts at about grid ref 246167. Combined with a trip to the tops, this outing provides a comparatively gentle (if sometimes damp) opportunity to explore a quiet aspect of the Borrowdale fells.

21. Gate Gill Grade 2 with Grade 3 options

Vertical Height: 270 metres: Guide time about 1 1/2 hours, but longer if the Grade 3 sections are included.

Care is required in wet conditions and the route is not recommended in high water. In poor conditions or if attempting the Grade 3 sections,

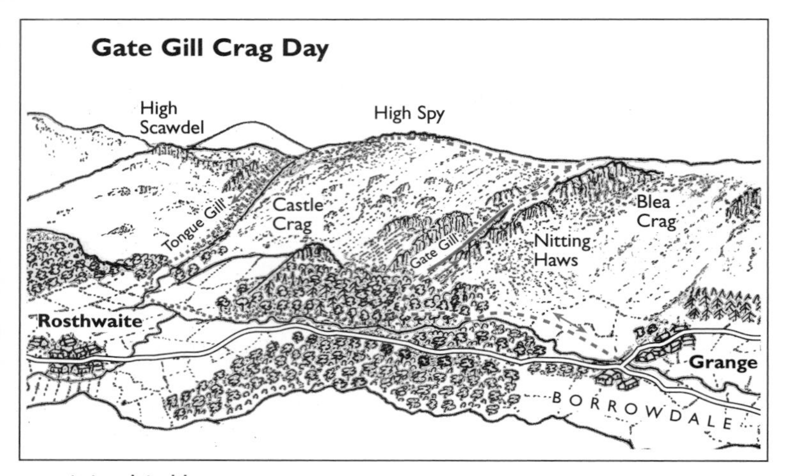

it is advisable to carry a rope.

Approach is from the small village of Grange. The Borrowdale Rambler bus stops by the bridge. If travelling by car, park in the small public car park by the bridge - if there's room, which there often isn't! There are laybys on the main road about 400m north, but these too are often full. There is also the larger Bowderstone car-park (pay and display) about 600m south. In a dry spell it may be possible to shorten the walk from here by fording the River Derwent.

Take the metalled track signposted to Hollows Farm and the campsite. Where the surfaced road turns right up towards the farm, take the left hand, rough track, which passes through the campsite. The main camping field lies on the right hand side above the trees. There is a stile at its top end. Cross this and follow the track uphill until it crosses a beck. This is Gate Gill.

Start from the path, and scramble up easy boulders in the stream bed to a tree-filled section of gorge where there is an overhanging block to right of the beck. This may be surmounted directly with some difficulty or passed more easily on its left, actually in the stream if water levels permit.

Water spills down a wide slab on the righthand side of the gill. The start, at the bottom right corner, is usually greasy, but the rock becomes much cleaner as you work up and left, crossing the main stream, to a small tree.

The stream now runs through a narrow slot, which is climbed on its right wall. Cross back to the water's edge and climb to a huge slab and easy ground.

Walk up the easy slabs, until you reach a steeper area of stepped slabs. These are climbed on their right, eventually bringing you to a very wet recess. Climb through the middle of the small cascade on good, clean holds to a second wet recess. Climb through this and follow dry rock with positive holds to reach a large holly tree. Climb the steep wall immediately to the left of the tree.

Scramble over boulders between steep walls, until the way is blocked by an unclimbable fall. This fall may be passed on its right at Grade 3, climbing mossy rocks and then a leftward slanting groove above a tree. However, it may be by-passed more easily by the grassy rake on its left. Either way, regain the stream immediately above the cascade. Climb a well-worn crack in the slab on the right.

There follows a long stretch of easy scrambling mainly over boulders. Interest is maintained by keeping as close to the main watercourse as possible, ascending little walls and cascades. This stretch finishes at a huge block which is passed by climbing a wall on its right.

Soon the ravine deepens and a small subsidiary stream cascades down a steep wall on the right. Climb a steep, clean central rib in the main bed and step across to the right wall, where holds are greasy but good, leading up to a tree. Move up and right about 6m then cross a series of ledges, back left to the top of the fall.

Bypass the next cascade on its left and return to the watercourse. Straddle another small cascade and follow the stream to another fall. This one is passed using holds and ledges in the right hand wall. Above it comes a section of huge boulder slabs, surmounted by a skeletal, dead juniper. Climb past this to an impressive fall cascading down a steep, dark cleft.

This can be climbed direct at Grade 3, but is extremely serious, except in extreme drought conditions, with slimy holds throughout and a guaranteed dousing in the second section. A steady nerve and a rope are recommended if this section is to be attempted. Alternatively, crawl through the juniper bushes to reach some clean ribs on the hillside immediately to the right of the ravine, which afford good views into the darkness below!

Regain the stream bed, where good scrambling remains, avoiding another unclimbable fall by grass ledges on the right, and ascending a stepped cascade on wet but very clean and positive holds. Soon after this the gill becomes a gentle beck bubbling through a rocky, heathery combe.

And Now?

Immediate descent can be made via a faint, steep path on the fellside to the right (north). It is more pleasant, however, to continue to the tops. Follow the faint path up the hill, hugging the side of the beck, then strike up its right-hand branch to meet the minor track that runs under Nitting Haws. Follow this up to the main ridge, with its well-worn trail and cairns. Turn left (south) to find the giant cairn on the summit of High Spy – about 45 minutes from the top of the scramble.

From here, take the descent path back to Borrowdale through the abandoned slate quarries and back along the side of the river to the campsite and the track to Grange – about 1 hour and 20 minutes.

Gillercombe Expedition

350m scrambling: 20m climbing: up to Diff

Gillercombe is one of the best examples in the Lakes of a hanging valley carved by a small subsidiary glacier. The floor of the combe is a tangle of moraine mounds and lurid bogs, from which Sour Milk Gill launches itself exuberantly down the steep side of the main Borrowdale valley. Gillercombe Buttress forms the combe's wall, and we finish with a short climb onto the very summit of Green Gable.

22. Sour Milk Gill

Grade: like the route, infinitely variable
Vertical height 200m: guide time 1 hour for unroped ascent by the easy ways

It's possible to find much entertainment in almost any conditions short of total spate. A good introduction to gill scrambling, while by seeking out harder variations it can be made much more challenging.

Approach from the farmyard at Seathwaite. Cars can be parked on the

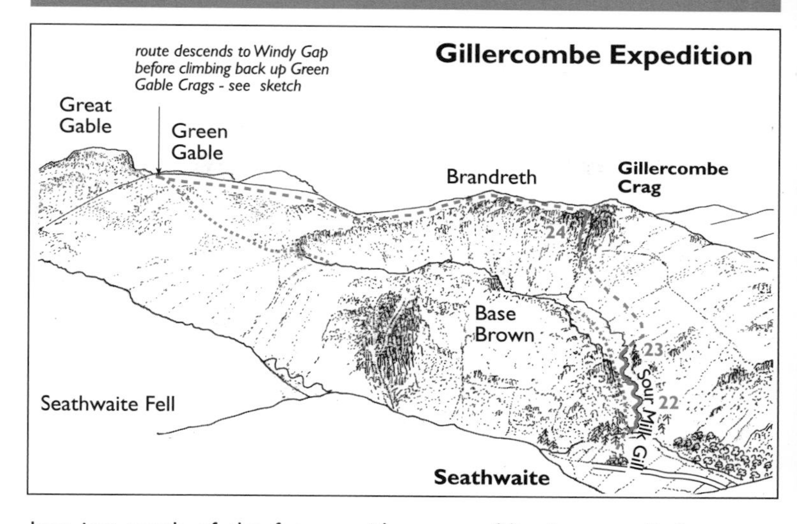

lane just north of the farm, or it's a mere 20 minutes walk from Seatoller, where the bus terminates. Go through the arch on the right, down a short lane and cross the Derwent on a footbridge. Go slightly right to a smaller footbridge over a tributary beck - this is Sour Milk Gill.

Start immediately from the footbridge at the foot of the gill. It's just easy boulder-hopping at first. There are two main channels for most of this lower section: keep between them, and generally favour the left one for best sport; the closer to the water the better. Trees variously help and hinder.

After nearly 100m of height have been gained, you reach a shady pool where the beck is concentrated into a narrow sluice. Go round to the left and make a tricky move to gain a fault-line parallel to the water: sidle along with feet at this level. Just above this a 5m fall is best taken on the left side.

Soon we come to the biggest cascade; above a steep lower section the stream is spread across slabs of black rock. Climb up on the right, on big holds close to the water. Above the black slabs there's a level shelf. If the water's low you can cross this and go up by a groove to left of the stream, but if it's high stay on the right.

Bernie Carter scrambling in Sour Milk Gill

The next feature is a narrow v-groove funnelling the entire gill. Climb up - a little earthy - to the right of a large birch tree. From the grass behind this climb an exquisite slabby rib. The rock is clean and rough as pumice. From the top of the rib slant back left to the bed of the gill. Traverse the next pool and climb up short walls to right of the next cascade. Keep on past more minor falls, through a gap in a stone wall, and so to the final fall, which drops free over a very steep wall. There's a detached pillar to its right (not a scramble!) and two trees on the left edge of the wall.

The best way is immediately left of the water but this is intimidating when there's a lot of it coming down. The soft option is to scrabble up an earthy groove well to the left and come back to the edge of the wall a few metres above the lower tree. Go up quite steeply but on great holds to the right of the upper tree. From here you can follow a shallow groove very easily to the top, or more boldly spider along the very brink of the wall. Either way you emerge abruptly onto almost level moorland.

Next: the walkers' path which descends to Seathwaite is just a few metres away to the left. Gillercombe Buttress is now very obvious

ahead. Off to the right are the clean planes of Seathwaite Upper Slabs.

23. Seathwaite Upper Slabs Grade 1 or 3

Vertical height: 20m: Guide time: 10 minutes

Cross the stream and go over a stile to reach the slabs. The blank-looking slab directly in front of the stile is not blank at all, but in its upper reaches the holds dwindle and it can feel precarious in big boots. It's good Grade 3 terrain. An easier line (Grade 1) lies a few metres to the left: start just to left of a grassy groove and finish by a rough crack in the upper tier.

Walk or scramble up to a rocky knoll above the slabs.

Next: Gillercombe Crag is just a short walk away across the boggy combe. A classic Severe route takes it head on, while our fine scramble is on a lesser buttress to the right.

24. Gillercombe Crag: North East Buttress Grade 2

Vertical Height 130m: guide time about 35 minutes.

A straightforward scramble with no major problems or route-finding difficulties, this provides a pleasant way to the fell tops. Much of this route shows the polished evidence of wear and tear, which is a great aid to route finding. This is because it incorporates sections of training climbs developed by the ubiquitous Bentley Beetham in the 1950s.

The main crag is bounded on its right by a gully, which drops from a grassy shoulder at about two-thirds height and has a broad scree fan at its foot. The grassy shoulder also forms the crest of a subsidiary buttress, up which the scramble makes its way. Above the shoulder it transfers onto the main crag.

Start at the lowest point of the easy-angled rocks to right of this scree. Vague but easy scrambling leads to the broad, easy-angled rib that forms the right-hand edge of the gully. Climb the rib, its excellent rock occasionally interrupted by heather, to a very obvious, clean, leftwards traverse ledge. Follow this left until once again close to the gully.

More slabs are climbed by a crack to a small recess, which leads left to a second, bigger recess. Scramble out from its left side to a shoulder just above, where you can pause to contemplate the much steeper section ahead.

For the easiest way up the steeper rock above, keep close to the gully at first then work back right, before moving left again to reach ledges which lead to the grassy shoulder above the gully.

Follow the ridge above, moving up below a short wall on the left. Ignoring the first crack that is encountered, proceed to a stepped break in the wall. Climb up though this weakness, and continue along the top edge of the wall to a point where two steep cracks, probably permanently green and wet, loom one above the other. Avoid these by traversing horizontally right to a big ledge. Launch yourself up a very smooth, steep but short corner. The feet may flail for a moment, but this will intensify the enjoyment of the excellent friction that follows as you continue to the top via the remaining rocks.

Next: a walk up the hillside of 5-10 minutes brings you to the main path near the Grey Knotts summit. Follow this over Brandreth to Green Gable.

Green Gable Crags

From here, various descents are possible (see And Now? after the next route). But best of all, top off the day with some climbing on Green Gable Crags. There is only one good climb here within the scope of this guide, Gamma, but this can be combined with Epsilon at a slightly harder grade (Mild Severe) to make an outing for which it is worth carrying the gear!

25. Gamma 70m Diff

Guide time including scrambling 1 hour.

The route is short but sweet, especially in the afternoon sun, and you are almost guaranteed to have it to yourself. Only 20m is roped climbing. First climbed in 1927.

Approach: From the top of Green Gable descend into Windy Gap, with fine views of the impressive Gable Crag - a very different beast from the sunny Napes on the other side of the hill - and contour right (north-west) under the broken crags below Green Gable's summit. Follow a faint path across scree to the lowest point of the crag, where there is a deep square cut chimney. Continue past this for about 20m to a grassy gully. Looking up this, Gamma can be identified as a clean, free-standing rib. Gain access to its foot by very careful scrambling up the gully for almost 50m on steep vegetation and some loose rock, eventually traversing right.

1. (20m) Climb the rib (via a ledge at about 10m) to its top. Easy scrambling leads back to Green Gable summit.

And Now? The most obvious descent is to retrace northward on the path used in the ascent, soon forking off rightward towards Base Brown and then branching left into Gillercombe. A steep and rocky descent alongside Sour Milk Gill leads back to Seathwaite.

Those who came by bus have a fine alternative covering much more new ground. Retrace as far as the col between Green Gable and Brandreth then drop left down easy slopes to a lower path - the celebrated Moses' Trod - which contours round the head of Ennerdale and then above Dubs Bottom on its way to Honister Pass. If, as is likely, the last Honister Rambler bus went hours ago, the old road provides an easy descent to Seatoller and the Borrowdale bus.

Langstrath Expedition: Cam Crag

The Scottish sound of the name is matched by a bare bleak feel unusual in Lakeland. The lower reaches of the valley are craggy, especially on the east side, but apart from West Face Route on Sergeant Crag, one of the most rambling of rambling Diffs, just about everything here is too hard. The valley has just one major offering for us, but it's a cracker.

Langstrath is reached from the hamlet of Stonethwaite, at the end of a short side-road just south of Rosthwaite. There is parking for four or five cars by the phone box. If this is full, backtrack to roadside spaces lower down. Cars should not be taken beyond the phone box unless staying at the campsite, pub or B&B. The Borrowdale Rambler bus stops at the end of the side-road, 5 minutes walk away.

26. Cam Crag Ridge Grade 2 (though scope for variation)

Vertical height almost 200m: guide time 1 hour for unroped ascent

The crux corner feels hard for the grade and it may be wise to use a rope (or avoid it).

From the approach this looks like a continuous ridge, but in reality it proves more episodic, rising in a series of steps. However, the steps are individually entertaining and the short walking sections don't break up the flow. It all adds up to one of the district's best-known scrambles, though it was first reported as a Moderate rock-climb in 1943 by Bentley Beetham.

The steep right wall is not matched on the left, where the ridge fades into the hillside, and therefore all the difficulties can be avoided, though this is no way to get the best out of it. The crucial corner can feel hard for the grade and should not be taken lightly.

Approach: From Stonethwaite follow the riverside, or the cart-track past the campsite, to the confluence of Greenup Gill and Langstrath Beck. There are some fine 'dubs' or swimming-pools in the beck here, below the steep nose of Eagle Crag and the excavated slabs of Bleak How. Continue easily up the valley, passing Heron and Sergeant Crags opposite. Eventually you reach a gate, roughly opposite the prominent Blea Rock. The ridge is now obvious up on the right. Cross the green 'field' slanting right, to a parting in bracken and then up to a boulder just below a detached outcrop. Ascend to left of the outcrop to a shelf immediately under the ridge, with a scattering of huge boulders. The walk up the valley takes about an hour.

Go up to the left of the boulders, and follow trodden steps up a shallow gully to the right of a block with a projecting holly-tree.

Start: the real scrambling starts at the top of the gully. Step right onto clean rock, up a couple of metres, step left then pull up right to a bare rock ledge. The best way now is straight up, with big flaky holds where it's steepest. Keep on up, more easily, on rough, bubbly rock to a grass ledge about 12m above the first rock ledge.

Continue at an easier angle, keeping as close to the right edge as possible. The ridge levels out and it's mostly walking to the next steep buttress.

A tongue of rock lies up against the base of the buttress, with a steep drop-off just to the right. Climb the tongue direct or, more easily, on either side, to a short but obvious - and steep - right-angled corner. This is the crux.

The holds are good but awkwardly placed, and the rock is smoother here, making it particularly disconcerting in the wet. At the top, the pull-out to the right is tricky too. Don't be embarrassed to take a belay and place a runner or two. And, as ever, the whole thing can be avoided by easy slabs on the left.

Above the corner, things soon ease to grass. The next buttress is also steep, with two obvious grooves. The one on the left is easier: step right as the angle begins to ease, for cleaner rock.

There's one more short rock-step, more walking, then a band of smooth rock, which is taken by a crack slanting up right.

Another short walk brings you to the foot of a 10m wall with pink mossy streaks. This is more broken than it first appears, but there are some loose blocks and the rock is smooth, so it's no joke when wet. It's best tackled from low on the right, first diagonally left, then straight up or back right into a little groove.

Walk on up to a friendly 5m wall, then walk some more to a fierce pink prow. This is skirted on the left by mossy slabs, moving back right. After a little more walking the final rock step is taken direct.

And Now?

Descent is possible either side of the crag, but easier on the left (north).

Alternatively, a short walk, bearing slightly left from the line of Cam Crag (general heading due west), leads to the head of Combe Gill. Turn left at the head of the Gill and head up onto Glaramara. The face of the fell has many small outcrops, inviting a pioneering scramble.

For a shorter way back to Borrowdale, walk north and then north-west to Tarn at Leaves. Just west of the tarn is a slight saddle and a very faint path slants down left from here. This becomes even fainter lower down but the slopes are broad and fairly open and a few zigs and zags lead down to the lower reaches of Combe Gill. If hungry for more rock, turn to the next page, and up left into the combe.

Combe Gill Crag Day

Variable amount of scrambling: 340m climbing: up to V. Diff

The little side-valley of Combe Gill rises quietly above the Honister road and gives easy access to two contrasting crags. Either is worthy of a visit in its own right, or they can be combined to make a day out on two of the best Diffs in Lakeland. For maximum sunshine, climb on Raven Crag in the morning and Dove's Nest Crag in the afternoon or evening.

In addition to the climbs the valley offers a wealth of good scrambles, and a pleasant day without roped climbing can be had by doing Intake Ridge, then dropping down to Dove's Nest Crag for the Attic Cave scramble (described by Brian Evans in *Scrambles in the Lake District*).

27. Intake Ridge Grade variable - from 2 to Diff

Vertical height almost 100m: guide time about 45 minutes for the easiest version, done unroped in dry conditions.

It was first reported in 1937, as a climb rather than a scramble, by Bentley Beetham. But a scramble it is, with lots of route choice, and the making of those choices is a large part of the fun.

Approach from the short branch road to Stonethwaite. Buses stop at the end of the branch road; cars can be parked nearer to Stonethwaite. Take a track at 257141 past the school and church and through Church House Farm. Where the path soon divides, take the left fork, up the hill-side, and continue along it until a gate takes you through a fine wall run-

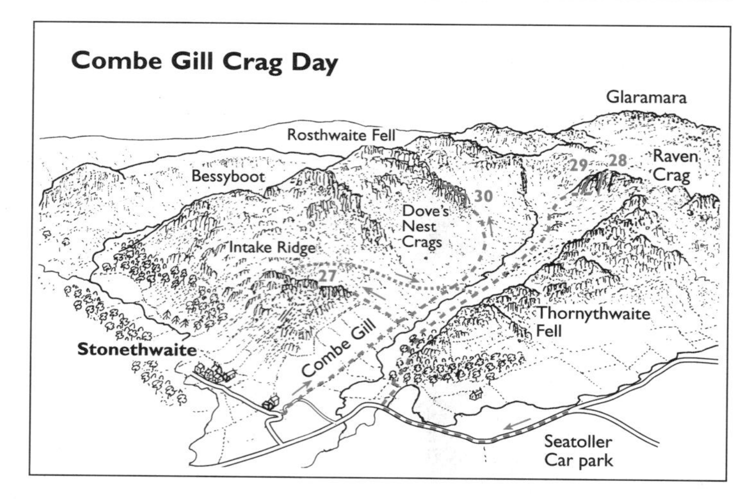

ning down the hillside (the intake wall).

Start: immediately through the gate, turn up left near the wall. The overall line is clear, and with so much scope for variation detailed description is unnecessary: use your own initiative.

The scramble works its way up the broken buttresses above the wall. If harder options are taken the route is Difficult, but all can be easily avoided.

Next: It is possible to continue up, over further scattered outcrops, to Bessyboot, but to enjoy more climbing, traverse right from the top of Intake Ridge to reach open slopes and descend back into Combe Gill. If Raven Crag is the next destination, descend straight down the slope and cross the stream where the main path lies close on the other side. For Dove's Nest Crag slant left as you descend and then contour to the left, just above the boggy floor of the combe.

Raven Crag

Approach: from the Seatoller car park and bus stop, walk back down the road towards Keswick for about 10 minutes. Turn off right onto the sign-

posted Thornythwaite access track, and turn off left after another 5 minutes along a good path that runs up into the Combe. The path climbs into the combe, and then the gradient eases briefly before it swings up and right, heading for Glaramara. At this point take a smaller path which forks off left, running almost level into the combe. This contours a little above the moraine mounds and bogs of the valley floor, finally climbing more

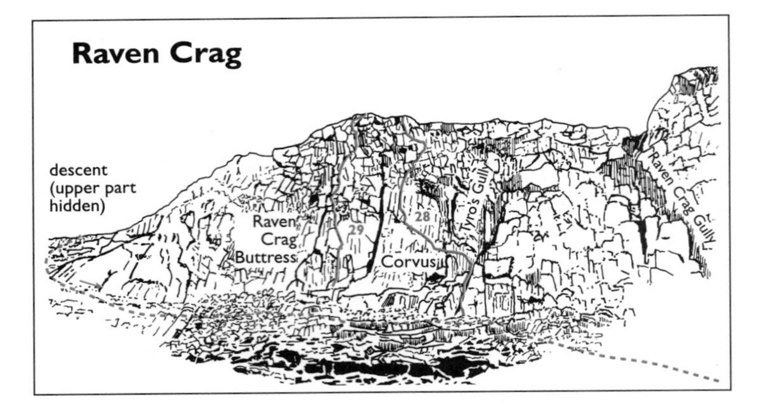

steeply up to Raven Crag, which dominates the back of the combe. The path is reasonably well-trodden and leads exactly to the start of Corvus - hardly surprising, as this one route must account for at least ninety percent of all ascents of the crag. Between 1 and 1 1/2 hours from the road.

Raven Crag presents a huge expanse of sometimes rather green rock, slashed by an obvious gully running its entire height. This is Raven Crag Gully, a frequently wet V. Diff. To the left of this is a narrower and shorter gully, Tyro's Gully. Just left again is the steepest and most impressive section of the crag. At the base of this section, running virtually its full width, is a level grassy shelf, with a further low tier of rock below it. Corvus starts at at the right-hand end of this shelf, and finds its way up the right-hand side of the steep section; Raven Crag Buttress starts at the left end of the shelf.

28. Corvus 150m Diff

Guide time about 2 1/2 hours

An absolute must and, with all respect for Giant's Crawl, a serious contender for the best Diff in Lakeland. The pitches are varied and route finding straightforward, following the clean and polished rock. It is slow to dry in damp conditions, otherwise the only drawback to an ascent of this fine route is the crowds. Get there early, mid-week or out of season!

First climbed in 1950 by that man Beetham again. It was probably then much more vegetated.

Start at the right-hand edge of a band of slabs, just to left of Tyro's Gully. Look for the all too obvious signs of a well-trodden route.

1. (23m) Climb the slabs, making a very polished and tricky move rightwards at the top of them to a ledge on the right. Go to the back of this to a chockstone belay actually in the bed of the gully.

2. (13m) Climb out of the gully again by a V-shaped cleft in the left wall. Stop immediately, to use sling and nut belays on the right of the stance.

3. (12m) Follow an obvious line of ledges, rising to the left, to belay below a corner.

4. (23m) Climb the corner and the chimney into which it turns, exiting left at the top. Climb a slab to a big recessed stance. Big nuts and medium hexes are useful for the belay.

5. (32m) Climb round the rib which forms the right wall of the recess and make a 10m easy traverse right, to reach the foot of another rib. (An intermediate belay is possible here). Climb all the way up the rib to belay at the bottom right corner of a steep slabby wall.

6. (10m) The celebrated Hand Traverse Pitch. The traverse is a line of flake handholds running to the left across the wall, which steepens above. You can reach its start up the right hand side of the wall; or, more directly but harder, by polished holds up the wall's centre. Once the flake holds are gained they are found to be big and comforting enough to allow acrobatic posing to impress the second. They lead naturally left to a set-back ledge.

7. (23m) Climb up the crack at the back of the recess to a large ledge. Climb a rib above, to belay below a scooped corner with an obvious large flake in it.

8. (14m) Ascend the slabby scooped corner on big flake holds, then climb on to the top of the crag, with an excellent thread belay.

Next: from the top of the climb move left (south) and into an obvious gully which leads down without too much difficulty. Where it opens out lower down, keep well to the right (now facing out) until it is possible to break back left below the crag. The descent passes below a clean slabby wall, almost detached from the main crag, which gives some harder single-pitch routes. Just to right of this and at the same level is the start of the grassy shelf, previously mentioned, from which Raven Crag Buttress starts.

29. Raven Crag Buttress 116m V. Diff

Guide time: 1 1/2 hours

Although initial impressions are that the route looks rather dirty, it is actually a worthy companion to Corvus or even an alternative if the queues on that route are too long. Historically it takes precedence, having been climbed in 1939. There are no prizes for guessing by whom.

Approach either from the descent as just described, or walk left from the start of Corvus.

Start from the left end of the grassy shelf above the foot of the crag, as previously described.

1. (33m) From the shelf, climb a deep squarish groove (not quite a chimney) and ascend several ledges above it, eventually reaching a deep recessed platform.

2. (27m) Initially climb a little leftward, then straight up, to a ledge perched above the gully which lies to the left. Continue fairly directly, passing a prominent flake, to a ledge stance.

3. (33m) From the back of the ledge, climb up a long groove-line, until a short corner leads to a large shrubby ledge.

4. (23m) Easy scrambling leads to the top.

Descent: as for Corvus

Next: across the valley, with an easy but very boggy walk between, lies

Dove's Nest Crag, somewhat smaller than Raven but appearing steeper and cleaner (appearances can sometimes be deceptive!) Allow about 30 minutes to walk between them across or around the bogs.

It is also possible, from the top of Raven Crag, to round off the day with a fellwalk over Glaramara. Strike directly up the hillside and the main path is soon met; follow this leftward to reach the summit in about 45 minutes. Options from Glaramara are described after the following route.

30. Dove's Nest Crag: Outside Route 75m Diff

Guide time about 1 1/2 hours

This is a fascinating route on a very unusual crag, offering a mixture of entertaining obstacles and something for every climbing style. Dove's Nest Crag was formed by a landslip that left massive slabs of rock lying against the fellside, creating a labyrinth of chimneys and tunnels as well as open slabs. About 20 years ago a further slippage of some of the rocks has rendered some of the routes unsafe. However, the route as described is solid.

Avoid alternatives, which involve more potholing at about V. Diff standard, through suspect rock.

The route was first recorded in 1944, by a party including Beetham, but had probably been climbed before.

Approach: from Stonethwaite, as for Intake Ridge, but once through the gate below that route continue straight ahead, into the combe, keeping to the left hand side of the beck. The crag is the most extensive piece of clean rock, rising above the scree near the head of the combe and not far above its floor. 1 - 1 1/2 hours from the road. Alternatively, approach from Raven Crag, as described above.

Start from the lowest point of the crag at a leftward trending, easy-angled crack.

1. (22m) Climb the crack to a big ledge on the left. From its right end ascend an arete heading for the bottom of a prominent chimney (North Chimney). Place a runner at the chimney's foot to protect the Second, then walk right, along the large ledge, to below the South Chimney – good thread belays (a 16-foot sling would be very useful!)

2. (8m) There is an extremely large detached block to the left of the belay. Unlikely as it seems, the next pitch climbs this on good holds, keeping to its right edge. Walk or teeter along its crest to take a belay at its far end and wonder where on earth the route goes next!

3. (13m) Lower yourself off the block and into the gully below (a sling can be left in place to protect the second if required, easily flicked off once the feet are firmly on the ground). Choose the big chimney in front of you. This is Central Chimney and is easier than its forbidding appearance suggests. Those with a long reach may climb it by keeping in front of the chockstones, but those without (and closet cavers) will need to squirm behind them. Belay on the topmost huge chockstone. The chimney widens just above to form the Attic Cave. A lower chock belay is possible if the rope's journey behind the chockstones has caused excessive drag.

4. (32m) The last pitch takes you back into the open air. From the belay take the left-hand rib (facing in) on easy holds for a couple of metres until a long stride across the chimney establishes you on the slabs on its right-hand side. Move slightly right and climb a fine crack, followed by a wider crack with good holds inside. From a pinnacle move left and up easy ground to the top.

Descent can be made, with care, down steep grass and rocky shelves on either side of the crag.

And Now?
A short but satisfying finish is to continue up the hillside to the little tor-like summit of Rosthwaite Cam at grid ref 257118, then work north and a little east to Tarn at Leaves. You can return to the lower end of Combe Gill from here (described in the Cam Crag page 91). To finish the day over Glaramara, head to the right, around the head of Combe Gill, with some scrambling to be found on outcrops below the summit.
From Glaramara, for a return to Seatoller take the westward path down the side of Hind Gill and thence out via Seathwaite - about 1 1/2 hours from the top. To return to Stonethwaite, drop down untracked hillside to the south-east, taking care to avoid rocky outcrops, to the main Langstrath path - probably nearer 2 hours.

A longer but very pleasant walk is to continue south-southwest over Allen Crags to Esk Hause, from where you can descend via Grains Gill to Seathwaite and Seatoller or down the full length of Langstrath to Stonethwaite - allow up to 3 hours either way.

Buttermere: Grey Crag Expedition

143m climbing: up to V. Diff, plus some scrambling to link the routes

Buttermere is a much-loved and much-photographed valley, with its two lakes backed by the scooped ridge of High Stile. It hides its rock-climbing high on that scooped hillside, in the fastness of Birkness Combe

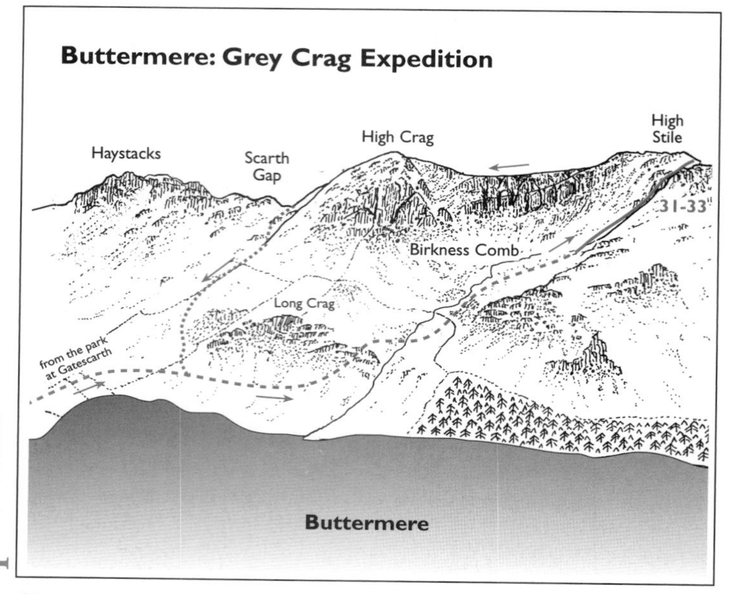

(Burtness Combe on some maps). Grey Crag has an open, friendly aspect, with many popular routes in the lower grades, and contrasts starkly with the massive, brooding Eagle Crag across the combe.

Access

Buttermere can be reached with ease from Keswick or Cockermouth. The best starting point for Grey Crag is Gatesgarth Farm, where parking is permitted for a reasonable fee. The access from Buttermere village is also straightforward, simply involving a longer walk around the west shore of the lake.

The Honister Rambler Bus services 77 (anti-clockwise) and 77A (clockwise) each make four departures daily from Keswick between late March and late October. With the first arrival in Buttermere at 0930, and the last departure at 1710, a day visit from Keswick is only feasible if you move fast on the hill, but for an overnight or longer stay the buses are very useful.

Amenities

Buttermere village has a campsite, two hotels and a café, with further camping available at Dalegarth, between Buttermere village and Gatesgarth Farm. The farm also has a campsite. There's a camping barn at Cragg and a YHA hostel, both on the periphery of Buttermere village.

Judith Brown on Oxford & Cambridge Direct

Grey Crag

Grey Crag is formed by a flight of buttresses rising from Birkness Combe. Its quick-drying rock offers a sequence of high quality climbs which runs right up to the summit ridge of High Stile against a backdrop of the lake below.

Approach from Gatesgarth Farm on the Buttermere - Honister road. Take the main track to Peggy's Bridge and start up the well trodden path towards Scarth Gap. At the first 'zig' strike out along a fainter track to the right. This leads in a rising traverse into Birkness Combe, which is entered by crossing the wall by a stile. There is a track along the bottom of the combe, though it is easily lost due to the boggy terrain. Follow the beck upwards until a trod leads up the screes to the lowest point of the crag. This is Harrow Buttress. About 1 hour 15 minutes from the car park.

Oxford &
Cambridge
Direct
start of
descent
33
Slabs
Ordinary
Route
32
scrambling &
walking link
Harrow
Buttress
31

31. Harrow Buttress 45m Diff

Guide time 45 minutes

An enjoyable route, readily protected with wires and slings and with good stances. While traditionally described with three pitches, 50m ropes enable this to be climbed conveniently in two. First climbed in 1912.

Start just left of the lowest point of the buttress.

1. (31m) Climb a well-polished, steep corner to a large ledge. Climb the chimney above, then make a short traverse left to a ledge below a broken groove. Climb this to easy, boulder-strewn ground below an overhung corner.

2. (14m) Climb the corner, pulling out to the left below the overhang, and follow easy rocks to the top of the buttress.

Next: follow a worn track slightly up and across rightwards into a narrow gully below a sweep of slabs. These slabs are part of Chockstone Buttress, the middle tier of Grey Crag. From the lowest point of the slabs, go up the gully for about 15m, to reach the start of an obvious rightwards traverse. This runs out horizontally and then a crackline rises to some perched blocks.

32. Slabs Ordinary 60m V. Diff

Guide time about one hour

An interesting route; originally done in 1913 it was abandoned after a serious rockfall and has not featured in recent guidebooks. In 2000 it was reclimbed, some remaining loose rock was removed, and the belay was relocated. It will reappear in the next edition of the Buttermere guidebook (publication date unknown). It provides open climbing to reach the foot of the top buttress.

Start: in the gully, at the foot of the traverse line already described.

1. (13m) Traverse horizontally right and then climb the crack and move onto and up the perched blocks to take a small spike belay on top of the

Climbers on Oxford & Cambridge Direct

uppermost block.

2. (28m) Climb up for 5m to a large sloping ledge. Climb the easy-angled rocks above to a short crack. Follow this and slabs above to belay at the bottom of a wide, open corner.

3. (20m) Climb the corner crack, which slants slightly left, then finishes more directly on good holds to the top.

Next: Immediately above is Oxford and Cambridge Buttress, which is composed of a fine steep wall, bounded on its left end by an arete. This arete divides the shorter left (south westerly) face from the fine, steep, right (north easterly facing) wall. The arete forms the final and hardest route of the three.

33. Oxford and Cambridge Direct 38m V. Diff

Guide time about 30 minutes if climbed in one pitch

This is an impressive climb, offering exposure and technical variety on clean rock with good protection. It's usually described in two pitches, but doing it in one makes the satisfaction even more intense. However, take the traditional midway stance if you don't like being a long way from your second on exposed and steepening rock. Surprisingly, the first ascent seems to be unrecorded.

1. (38m) From its lowest point, climb the arete on its right hand side, then move to its left, before making a steep pull onto its crest and climbing to a ledge about 15m up (possible intermediate belay). Move up left from the ledge to a bulging crack, which is climbed with difficulty, then move back right towards the arete and a ledge. Continue up the right edge, surmounting a further off-putting bulge by locating the 'Thank God' hold above, and then to the top and substantial belays.

And Now? Descent to the bottom of the crags is by following a narrow, well-trodden gully on the right (facing out) to the foot of Oxford and Cambridge Buttress, then traversing right into a wider scree gully. By going well to the right it is possible to keep to a more grassy descent, avoiding the badly eroded scree. (About 15 minutes back to the toe of Harrow Buttress).

However, it is much more satisfying to continue to the top of the ridge (5-10 minutes) for a fine ridge-walk over the summit of High Stile and down to Buttermere from Scarth Gap; or even on over Haystacks and Fleetwith Pike to make it truly a mountaineering day. You can find some nice scrambling on the way up Haystacks if you take it direct, spurning the new pitched path.

Helvellyn & Fairfield

The fells east of Dunmail Raise are better known for winter routes than for summer rock-climbing. In fact there are a number of fine steep crags, but long valley approaches mean they are rarely besieged by crag-rats. The area also has masses to offer the scrambler. The east side of Helvellyn sports two of the district's best known rock ridges, Striding and Swirral Edges. These don't really qualify for inclusion in this book, though in winter conditions the circuit of the two is a grand mountaineering day out.

Time-consuming approach walks, especially on the eastern side, and long, sweeping ridges above, mean that a scramble in this section is best taken as just one part of a long fell day. The Deepdale routes give scrambling ascents from valley to ridge. Pinnacle Ridge, on St Sunday Crag, is one of the most sought-after scrambles in the Lakes. The heftiest dose of scrambling is on the relatively unsung crags of Brown Cove.

Access

Main roads run down both sides of the range. The main bus route through the district (555 LakesLink) runs along the A591 below the western flank, providing good access throughout the year. On the eastern side, Patterdale is served by bus 517 (Kirkstone Rambler) which

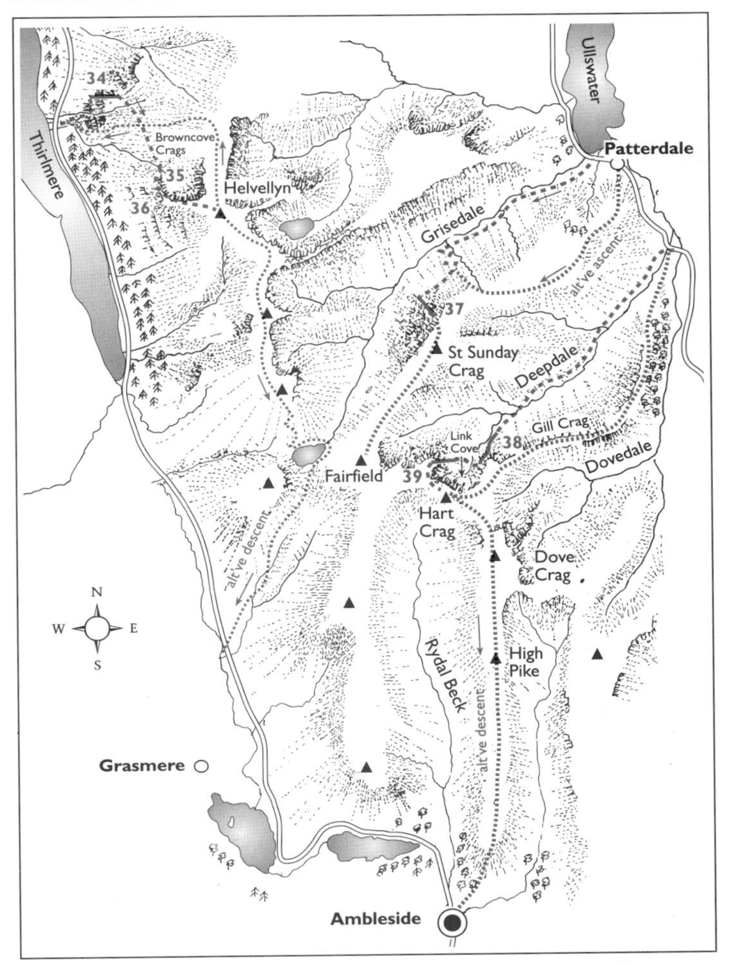

links Bowness, Windermere and Glenridding. This runs on Saturdays, Sundays and bank holidays from early April, and then daily in high summer. There's a year-round bus (no. 108) from Penrith to Patterdale.

Amenities

For Brown Cove on the western side, Keswick and Grasmere are the nearest centres, but neither is within reasonable walking distance of our scrambles. The nearest accommodation is the King's Head pub at Thirlspot and the much grander Dale Head Hall. There's a campsite near the King's Head, and another a kilometre to the north. There's also a scattering of B&B accommodation, but no longer a youth hostel at Legburthwaite.

On the eastern flank the principal bases are the villages of Patterdale and Glenridding. Each of these has plenty of hotels and B & B's, as well as a campsite and a youth hostel. The Patterdale hostel is on the main road south of the village while the Glenridding one is in the valley of the same name, a couple of kilometres west of the village. There is also a camping barn nearby. Additionally, there is a popular campsite, bunkhouse and pub at Brotherswater, just below Kirkstone Pass.

Helvellyn Crag Day

390m scrambling up to Grade 3

The traveller on the A591, especially coming from the south, gets the impression that the west side of Helvellyn is one vast uniform slope. In fact the best scrambling on the range is on this side, in the large open combe of Brown Cove. The crags here are both larger and better than they appear from a distance. Unfortunately, the approach doesn't quite measure up. The main Helvellyn path is comparatively brief but very boring. A natural route is by Helvellyn Gill, but there's not a vast amount of scrambling on it. The suggested approach via Whiteside Gill is more devious but offers rather more rock.

34. Whiteside Gill Grade 1

Vertical height about 120m: guide time about 30 minutes

A slight scramble, but still quite a bit more interesting than trudging up the main path.

Approach: Start from North West Water's car park at Swirls, just north of the forests that line the main road along Thirlmere. The bus stops

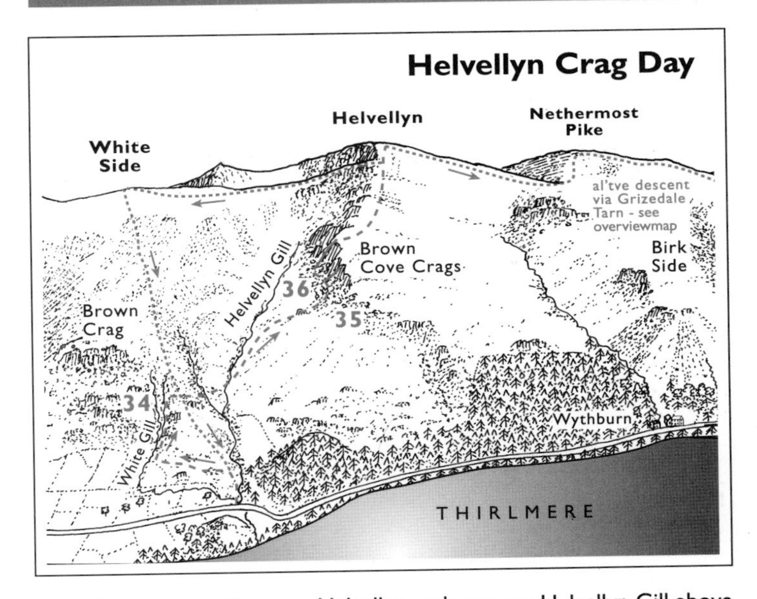

near the entrance. The main Helvellyn path crosses Helvellyn Gill above the car park, and goes up just left of the beck. Where this main path crosses back, go round to the left and follow a path just above a wall. After about 400m this crosses Whiteside Gill at another footbridge.

Start from the footbridge. Follow the gill at first, as closely as water levels permit, until you need to duck under juniper and holly into a dark recess. Either of the two watercourses ahead may be climbable at Grade 3 in drought. Failing this, the prudent plan is to escape right directly opposite a large larch tree - and perhaps aided by its branches. Immediately above the obstacle, traverse back in to the stream bed, with care. Continue, as near to the water as possible, for about 100m horizontal distance, to arrive at a steeper step. This is usually climbed by a break about 4m right of the fall. Now for a long stretch it's more boulder-walking than scrambling. Just above two trees, the stream runs over water-washed slabs, tricky when slippery. Above is a steeper step, with sound rock but sloping holds. If this is greasy and you don't fancy

Bernie Carter scramblng up Whiteside Gill

climbing it in socks, avoid it by breaking out on the right. Come back in above, or else climb rocky ribs on the open hillside further right.

Next: that ends the scrambling in the gill so angle right, with a few more rocky outcrops of mild interest. Brown Cove Crags are visible, still far off and considerably higher. Slogging diagonally across the slope towards them gets you into wet rough ground, so it's better to go directly uphill to find a path about 150m higher. Not totally clear in places, this runs almost level across the hillside, then kicks up slightly where it overlooks the left branch of Helvellyn Gill. The path now winds up to the lip of the combe below Brown Cove Crags.

There are two scrambles here. The best plan is to climb Stepped Ridge first, especially as Central Buttress finishes higher up the mountain. Damp conditions will make the routes noticeably harder, though not impossible.

35. Brown Cove Crags: Stepped Ridge Grade 2

Vertical height about 120 metres: guide time about 40 minutes for unroped ascent

It's difficult to work out a satisfactory scrambling route low down, but the upper reaches coalesce into a fine airy ridge that's most enjoyable.

Approach: Either from Whiteside Gill as described, or take the main Helvellyn path and follow the right branch of Helvellyn Gill up into the combe. Faint paths wander up towards the looming crags. Stepped Ridge is obvious, to right of the dividing gully and the first steep section of crag as you approach.

At its base are two tiers of very steep rock. Even the easiest route up the first - a left-slanting ramp near the right side - is precarious, especially when damp. Rock-fall has altered the established scramblers' route up the left side of the second tier. There are definite possibilities for roped climbs here, however.

The best plan for cautious scramblers is walking or scrappy scrambling up to the right of both tiers, to reach a sloping grass terrace above the second.

Start: at the left-hand end of this terrace. Move up, near the gully on

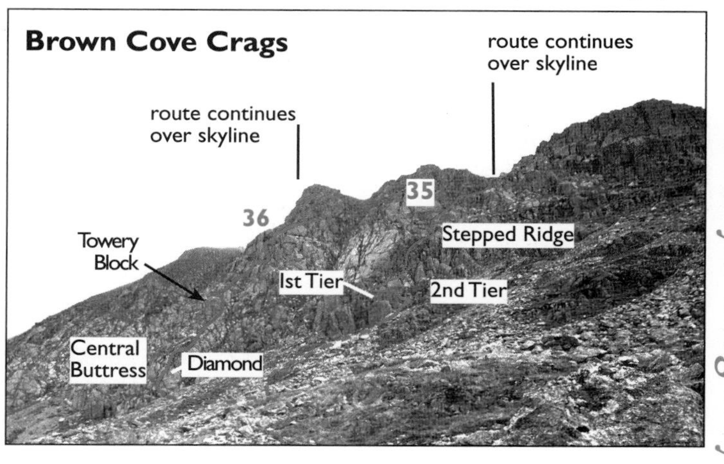

the left, to some fine clean rock steps. The first two of these are steep, and good Grade 3: they can be avoided by easier scrambling on the right. The lover of strenuous moves, however, can take the first step by its steep central crack. Above this is a large sloping rock ledge and then the steep wall of the second step. This is best started from near the right edge of the ledge, and climbed near its right-hand edge. Again this is quite dynamic - once begun, it's hard to reverse - and the exit has some shattered rock.

Above another, smaller step the ridge narrows. The best way is straight on up the apex, using a flake-crack with crampon scratches. It's very steep but the holds are good. Above a grassy section pick a line up the more broken step above.

The next step is awkward. The best plan, though not easy, is to climb the quartzy slab about 10m to the right of the edge above the gully. Come back left towards the gully, step off a block onto a small hanging slab and climb up past another block to a grassy neck.

Move left below a large hanging block and climb an awkward crack on the left side of the next, lesser block. Beware loose rock at the exit. Go up to the left of the next steep nose for about 5m and then climb over blocks straight up onto the crest. Follow this to a nice grassy saddle with a fine view, secluded from the crowds on the Helvellyn path.

Descent: The gully which splits the crag makes for an uncomfortable descent, with some slippery slabs lurking. It's less nerve-racking to follow the busy path downhill (back towards Swirls) until you can traverse back into the combe through a boulder-field.

36. Central Buttress Grade 3

Vertical height about 150 metres: guide time about 45 minutes for unroped ascentLarge rucksacks may prove awkward at one point, in which case a short rope or a few slings may be useful for hauling. Solo scramblers may find this very awkward: better to carry a small sack!

A fine, if slightly episodic, scramble up an extensive buttress.

Approach from the previous route, or directly into the combe. Pass below Stepped Ridge and cross a grassed-over scree fan. The principal features of the lower half of the buttress can be identified from this area:

a diamond-shaped slab below a steep wall, then a long rib which runs up to the right side of a steep towery block.

From the scree fan cross barer scree, with lots of parsley-fern, aiming for the diamond-shaped slab.

Start: At the left side of the scree fan, below the diamond, there's a small cairn marking the start of the route.

Climb a slabby rib slanting left and continue up left, skirting the left side of the diamond slab, then head back right, up clean stepped rock to a break above the diamond. Go left round the end of a steep wall, then move up and right onto an easier-angled rib. Go straight up this long but discontinuous rib towards the right side of the aforementioned towery block. The final steps are pleasant, with quite steep moves on good holds. The rib ends abruptly, with a grassy gully above.

Although not obligatory, it's most entertaining to move left along an exposed narrow ledge just below the top of the tower, then straight up easy rock to a grassy platform. The grassy gully also leads to this point. Go uphill and to the right, on grass, to the foot of another steep tower which has a block sitting on its top. On the right, immediately below the tower, is a collection of large jumbled blocks. Step to the right below these, and climb a slanting crack filled with a necklace of small chockstones. As this peters out, climb an easy slab then head leftward on steep rock with good holds to reach a small recess just to right of the impressive tower.

Climb the back right corner of the recess to squeeze through the hole under a perched block. Getting in is awkward while getting out is unnerving. Large rucksacks may need to be removed and could easily jam when being hauled, so one person should remain to guide them from below. Above this, scramble up to just below a large triangular perched block, then walk right for a few steps to the next band of steep rock.

After one awkward step, move up more easily into a recess below a kind of gully formed by twin grooves. Start up the right-hand one for a couple of metres then step left into its partner. Climb to grass which slopes up left, and continue up this to another perched block, which makes a good rest spot.

Move up a few metres then go to the right across a steep grass patch and up steep cracks onto an arete. Climb this for 5m then move across the grassy gully on the right to a large boulder speckled with quartz. The very brave can climb straight up the steep rock above, by a corner crack, but its right side is a pillar that looks as if it could collapse at any time. It's more prudent to go a little further right, below the pillar, before climbing up, trending slightly right. Here the rock is less bad, though still somewhat shattered.

Finish up less continuous rocks: these are very shattered in places but not too exposed. Finally you reach a level grassy ridge which joins the Helvellyn path.

And Now?

Anyone with a drop of mountaineering blood in their veins will want to continue to the summit of Helvellyn. Keep to the edge of the combe for the best views. It's about a kilometre to the summit, with about 100m of ascent.

Rather than returning straight down the path to Swirls, it's more interesting to head over Helvellyn Lower Man to Whiteside. You have several options from here, one being to descend due west on easy grassy slopes until you meet the path, encountered earlier, above Whiteside Gill. You can continue directly down from here, though care is needed as there are outcrops where the slope steepens, or follow the path north to Thirlspot and the bar of the King's Head.

Those who aren't tied to a car have an even better alternative: walk south over Nethermost Pike and Dollywaggon Pike then descend to Grisedale Tarn. After a short ascent to Grisedale Hause, Tongue Gill's path leads naturally down into the bar of the Traveller's Rest, or to the main road, with a bus stop just below the pub.

St Sunday Crag Expedition

37. Pinnacle Ridge Moderate (Grade 2 if the crux is avoided)

Vertical height 150m: guide time an hour or more for sensible scramblers belaying the crux

St Sunday Crag looks across the gulf of Grisedale to the scalloped eastern flank of the Helvellyn range. A series of ridges offer short rock-climbs

on the steep lower reaches, with scrambling routes above. Pre-eminent among them is Pinnacle Ridge, the best-known of Lakeland's true, wild scrambles. Admittedly, its popularity means that it isn't as truly wild as it used to be but there are still many good reasons for seeking it out. More than any other scramble in the Lakes, Pinnacle Ridge offers - albeit briefly - the feel of an Alpine crest. That crest is also extremely photogenic, and is one of the reasons for the route's popularity. For once a late start is rewarded: photographers will find the light at its best late on a summer afternoon.

However, this is not a route to take lightly. The crux corner is frequently greasy and even when dry is a spiteful piece of climbing, while the ridge above is very exposed. It should also be noted that the lower section, in particular, is composed of large stacked blocks, and care should be taken in assessing their stability.

The climactic crest is a good place to practice the Alpine skills of moving together. The natural threading of the rope through the maze of blocks provides a measure of protection on the opening and closing passage, but it's worth carrying a few proper runners, and switching to belayed climbing, for the crux.

While the scrambling is superb, the time spent on it is relatively short

Exposed scrambling on Pinnacle Ridge

compared to the approach and descent. You could descend - if you can find the way! - to do other scrambles on the crag (see Evans: *More Scrambles in the Lake District*).

The route was first climbed, and graded Moderate, on January 1st 1955. This remains a fair grade for the crux pitch in good conditions. Many competent climbers who thought this a good route for an 'off-day' have had a nasty shock.

Approach from Patterdale. There is limited parking on the side road which leaves the A592 near Patterdale church; if this is full, cars must be left in Patterdale village. Follow the lane up into Grisedale; or, from Patterdale village, take a path that starts behind the Patterdale Hotel and winds above the intake walls to Thornhow.

Follow the Grisedale valley track past Elmhow farm, to the end of the plantation just beyond. Go up the side of this and round to the left, then up the left side of a small outcrop to pick up an old, grooved, zig-zag path. This leads up to the lip of Blind Cove.

A devious but more interesting route to Blind Cove is over Arnison Crag and then via the upper reaches of Coldcove Gill. Skirt rightwards

round Gavel Moss to the col between St Sunday Crag and Birks, from where it's a short, rough descent into Blind Cove. You could also start from Deepdale (see next chapter) with some easy (Grade 1) scrambling in Coldcove Gill on the way.

From the lip of Blind Cove, follow a reasonably distinct path rightwards across boggy ground, then threading some moraine mounds. Continue another 300m across bouldery slopes, then cross a tongue of scree. About 50m further on is a narrow run of finer scree. Plough up the steep slope alongside this on its right. Looking up, there is a small tree in a v-notch on the skyline, with a rock tower just to its right and then an obvious finger of rock just right again. Tree, tower and finger are landmarks on the central part of Pinnacle Ridge.

The treadmill ends just below the level of more continuous rock. An hour and a half from Patterdale.

There are three distinct areas of clean slabs, with a broad gully between the middle and right-hand ones. There's a cairn below the right-hand edge of the right-hand slab-sweep.

Start at the cairn. Begin in a slight gully above the cairn, but break out right as soon as possible, over blocks and flakes. Paths weave through and around this section but the right edge, overlooking the gully, soon becomes quite exposed.

The 'finger' is now seen as a clean, leaning slab. Go up over blocks to its base and then shuffle to the right. Continue up more easily - it's hard to avoid using the path - until stopped by a steep tower. Walk round its left side and up into the recess behind.

Now the crux: starting in the very back of the recess, climb the steep crack up the left wall. Although the holds are generally good, they are polished and often greasy as well - a bad combination. The exit onto ledges is cause for great relief. If the crux is particularly greasy, or you just don't fancy it, it can be avoided: make an unpleasant descent into the gully on the left, then go up the heather slope on its left. Traverse back across the gully a few metres above a substantial rowan tree, to regain the ridge at the ledges above that sometimes-greasy crack.

Above the ledges, there's another steep step, which is climbed on its left side. Next comes the famous, photogenic - and all too short - spiky crest. At the end go down the right-hand (as you face St Sunday Crag) side of the ridge, with some awkward moves, onto a slab; and then move further right across it to a notch where the ridge runs into the main fell-side.

Climb out of the notch to an open slope, with another section of clean steep rock above. Start just left of its lowest point and climb fairly directly up. The final short wall will bamboozle many, especially shorter scramblers: it can be avoided on the left but does make a nice abrupt finish.

And Now?

Simply continue up the open slope above, bearing right to the summit of St Sunday Crag, which is further away than you think. The continuation to Fairfield is a very pleasant ridge walk, with a steep rocky section (though no serious scrambling) at Cofa Pike.

Deepdale Expedition

200m scrambling up to Grade 2: about 70m of this can be replaced with V Diff climbing

Deepdale is, as its name suggests, one of the longer and lonelier valleys

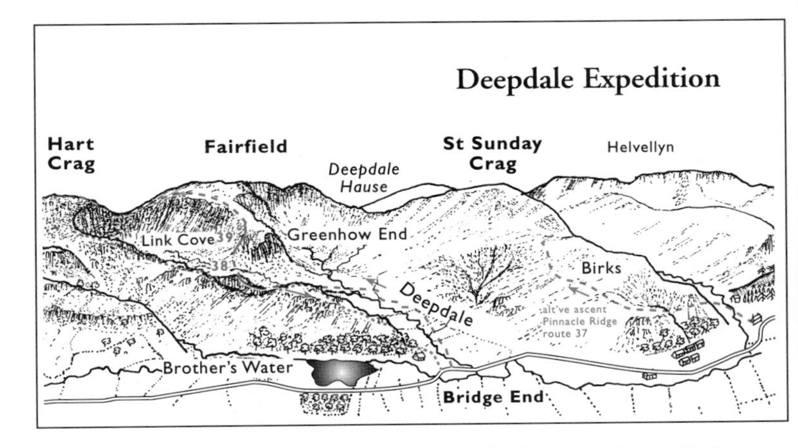

of the eastern fells. Two scrambles can be linked here, in increasingly impressive surroundings, to reach the ridge of Fairfield. The swarms of Fairfield Horseshoe walkers at the top come as a bit of a shock after the quiet of Deepdale.

38: Link Cove Beck Grade 2 for the soft options: V. Diff (wet) for the direct route

Vertical height about 100m: guide time about 30 minutes for unroped ascent by the soft options, at least 1 1/2 hours for the direct route

A route with a split personality. As a true gill route it's a climb, rather than a scramble, and a wet one at that. If the water is high, or for those who don't want a wet rock-climb, there is a fair amount of rock flanking the beck on the right and this makes a reasonable - and reasonably dry - scramble, though even this gets distinctly meaner in wet weather.

Approach

The usual starting point is Bridgend, where the A592 crosses Deepdale Beck. It's an easy walk of about an hour up Deepdale to an area of moraine mounds. As the main path rises steeply up the front of one of these, look for an indistinct path slinking off to the left. It keeps close to the beck for a little longer, then crosses it and winds up to the foot of the steep, tree-filled ravine of Link Cove Beck.

Start at the foot of the first rocky cascade. The first section is an obvious open cascade: climb dry rock to its left. There's a more broken section between two branches of the stream, which leads to a pool in the first shady ravine section.

The direct route traverses the left wall, close to the water, and then goes up the cascade to the right of a large boulder. Otherwise, climb the rocky rib on the right, overlooking the pool.

The next fall presents a rock climb that is probably of at least Severe standard even in drought. It's worth dipping into the bed of the gill to take a look at it. Escape by a break in the right wall and up a groove and slabs on the right.

At this point you choose between the wet climb and the dryish scramble. For the climb, return to the gill bed near the top of this fall - unpleasantly near, in fact. The moves down and along are exposed at first and feel insecure, especially if damp. This traverse leads into another narrow cleft and pool. The traverse of the left wall is usually slimy and then there's a choice - an awkward groove, with improving holds, or the fall itself.

Above is an amphitheatre with a larger waterfall at its back. The next pitch is the crucial one. It offers no easy escape and its protection is poor. Assuming you don't choose to climb the waterfall from its foot, the steepening slab to left of the water runs out of good holds as you go up, and in the end you're forced into the watercourse anyway at the lip of the fall.

If none of that appeals - which is no disgrace - open slabs to the right of the ravine offer a pleasant alternative. Traverse back to the gill just above the level of the main fall.

The next section is friendlier, and you can climb steep grooves just to right of the stream or rough slabs further to the right again. Above most of the trees there's another cascade, which can be climbed direct, but if you've stayed dry so far it's reasonable to climb the rocks on its right side. Above this the best rock lies between the two branches of the beck.

Another cascade lies below some more rowan trees. This is usually greasy, and can be avoided on the right. There's one more small fall, for

On the open scrambling at the start of Link Cove Beck

which the only dry option seems to be grass on the right, and that's about it.

39. Greenhow End Grade 1, with scope for harder moves

Vertical height about 100m: guide time about 15 minutes, depending on where you think it ends.

In contrast to Link Cove Beck, this route offers open scrambling on clean, rough rock, and should be possible in most weathers. It's one of the best, yet least-trodden, ways onto Fairfield.

Approach from the previous route: anything else is too much like hard work. The broad rocky face of Greenhow End looms above on the right. Slant up towards its foot, crossing a lesser stream. Aim for the lower left

side of the face, to left of a grassy rake which provides a walkers' route (not, apparently, a heavily used one).

Start: there's a swathe of light-coloured slabs to left of the grassy rake, with a band of steeper, darker rock at the base. Start a few metres to the left of a small tree which grows at the base of the darker band.

Begin to left of the tree, then move right to climb the steep section directly above it, on good holds, to a grassy break.

The lighter slabs above are climbable just about anywhere; the most continuous rock will be found by angling first right and then back left. Above them there are tiers of darker, bubbly rock, which invite the scrambler to play. There's plenty more fun to be found until the angle eases back into the ridge above.

And Now?

Aspirant Alpinists could reverse the scramble - good practice in descending. However, a rewarding walk can be had by following the ridge - still rocky in places - above Hutaple Crag, and then bearing left to swing round above Scrubby Crag. Continue fairly level until you meet the eroded scar of the Fairfield Horseshoe path. Follow this down to Link Hause and up a short rise onto Hart Crag. As it levels out look for a smaller path bearing away left, to take you down the neat ridge of Hartsop above How.

If you started the day with a bus ride from Ambleside you could also follow the main ridge (eastern arm of the Fairfield Horseshoe) on over Dove Crag and High and Low Pikes to Low Sweden Bridge. From here Nook Lane runs straight down to the front door of the Golden Rule.

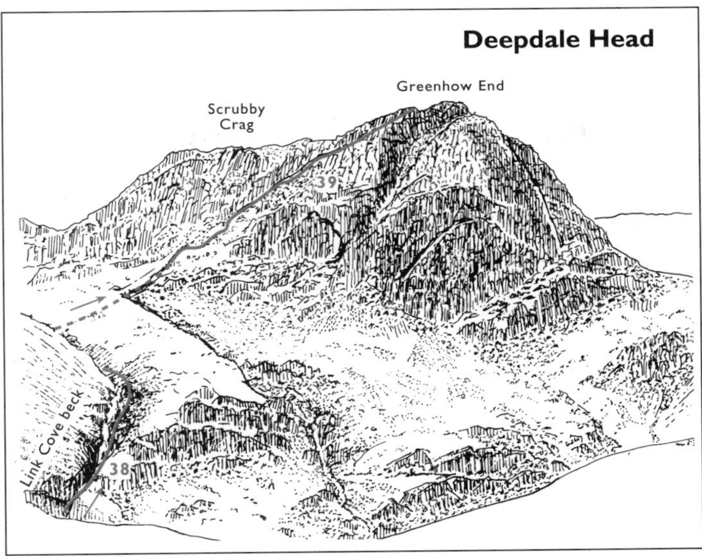

Bernie Carter on the pleasant slabs of Greenhow End

Coniston Fells & Duddon Valley

The Coniston Fells are a distinct group, semi-detached from the rest of the high fells; in views from the south they often appear higher than anything else. They look down over the long ribbon of Coniston Water and, gleaming in the distance, the wide expanse of Morecambe Bay. On their west side is the green and sheltered valley of the Duddon.

Their geology is mixed and interesting. Veins of copper and other

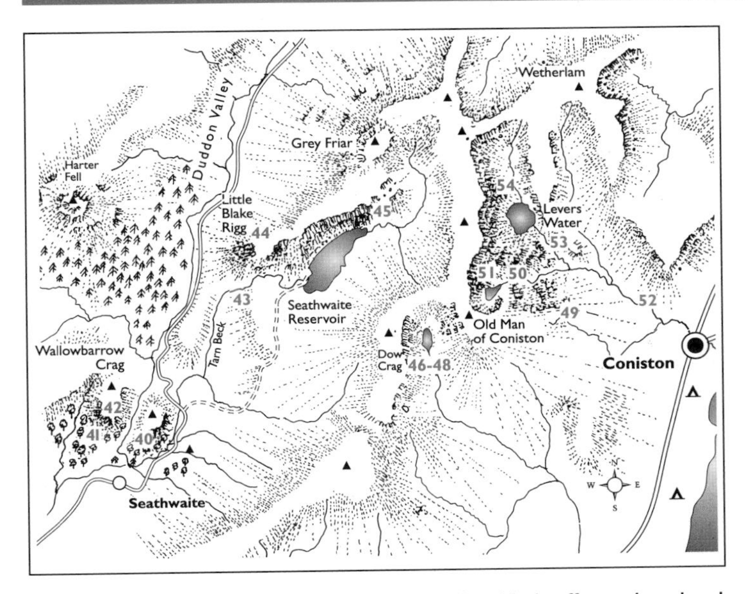

minerals wriggle through these hills. Bands of welded tuffs produce hard slate for construction and roofing - much of Coniston village is built of it. The uncommercial rock that remains - and there is a vast amount - is a rich resource for the scrambler, offering long expeditions from valley to ridge. There is much more to do than we can describe here.

Where so much is good, the very best is Dow Crag. It is one of the most accessible of the high mountain crags of the District, one of few to stand above a tarn, and one of few to lie directly below a mountain summit. Oddly, Dow has rarely, if ever, been at the cutting edge of climbing standards. But then, it has never been out of fashion either. Surely that is what is meant by 'classic'.

Just a few hours' walk away to the west, the Duddon Valley feels almost forgotten; it is one of the least commercialised corners of the district. It's a place to climb in quiet surroundings, comfortably close to the road. The scrambling doesn't lend itself to continuous expeditions, but there is plenty of it, and mostly on rock that is rough, accommodating, and angled to the afternoon sun.

Access

Coniston village has bus links with Ambleside and Windermere (service 505) and also with Ulverston (service X12). The Ulverston buses pass through Torver, which is a good alternative starting point for Dow Crag and even for Low Water above Coniston. Windermere is the terminus for Lakes Line trains, and Ulverston is on the Furness Line.

Sadly, public transport in the Duddon valley is non-existent apart from a postbus that takes several hours to reach Seathwaite. Those without cars are limited to hitching from Broughton-in-Furness, or walking over the hill from Coniston. The Walna Scar Road is damaged by four-wheel drive vehicles, and a quieter crossing is from Torver, by tracks curving south of Caw. For the motorised, there is limited parking near Seathwaite Church, and more at Wallowbarrow Farm (payment by honesty box).

Amenities

Coniston is not a centre on the scale of Ambleside or Keswick, but it does have restaurants, a food shop, a gear shop, a bank, and a range of accommodation. There are campsites at Coniston Hall and Park Coppice.

Of the pubs in the village, the Sun Inn is the first on the way down from the fells, and very pleasant too. Beer connoisseurs will probably head for the Black Bull, which brews its own ales including the award-winning Bluebird Bitter, but does get very crowded. Both are endorsed by the Good Pub Guide. The two pubs in Torver, the Wilson's Arms and the Church House Inn, can also be recommended.

The Duddon valley has a small shop and post office at Ulpha, a scattering of B & B's, and a campsite at Turner Hall. It also has the Newfield Inn, one of the best pubs in the Lake District (and therefore in the whole wide world).

Duddon Valley Crag Day

105m of climbing, up to V. Diff

The Duddon Valley has no lake, and nor does it claim ownership of any major peak. Its charms are more subtle. For the climber, the main attraction is Wallowbarrow Crag: low-lying and sunny, it offers the rare treat of a valley crag that isn't beset by road noise. This itinerary is a little contrived, but if it means a day pottering about on south-facing rocks in one

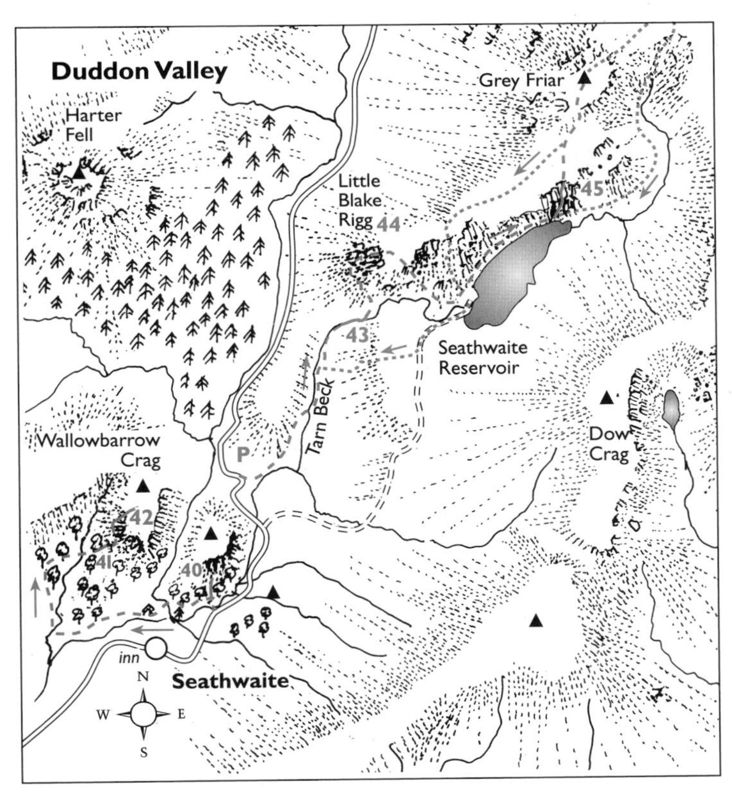

of the most idyllic of Lakeland settings, who cares? The arboreal start of the first route can hold moisture; otherwise they all dry quickly.

40: Seathwaite Buttress: Snap 30m Diff

Guide Time 40 minutes

A route of real character. The primitiveness of the first pitch just adds to the lustre of the rest. First climbed in 1956.

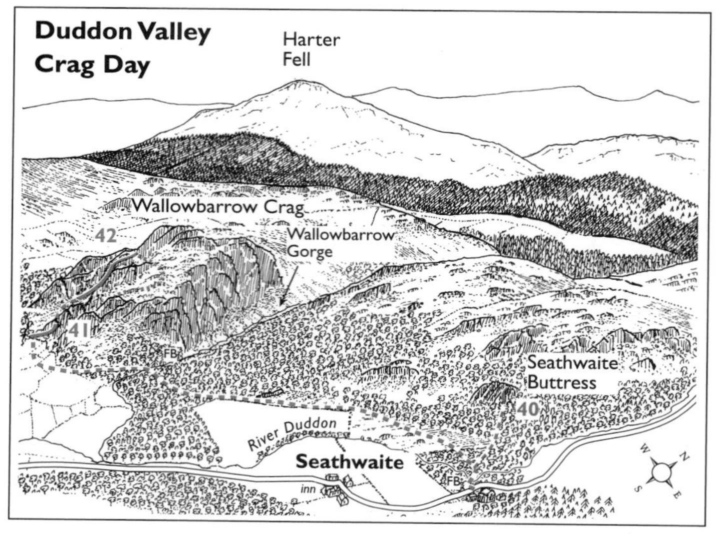

Approach: almost opposite Seathwaite Church is a footpath sign. Follow the path round to, and over, a footbridge and stick with it until it curves away from the beck near some old sluices. Leave it here, forking off right onto a narrower path which starts near the beck. This gets clearer as it climbs gentle slopes, initially alongside a stone wall, to the crag.

Start just to left of the lowest point, where a bulging oak tree grows just above the base of the crag.

1. (7m) Do a Tarzan impression up the side of the oak tree, then scramble up to the holly and belay. (Doing the whole route in one pitch will lead to problems with rope-drag.)

2. (23m) Climb twin cracks and continue up much cleaner rock for a few metres, before moving right to a wide crack/chimney formed by a huge detached flake. Climb the crack, and then the wall on its left, to reach the top of the flake. This provides a stance you could hold a party on, but no decent belays. Move up and right to a block on the right-hand (east) face of the crag, and make an awkward final move with a faceful of heather.

Descent: move up a little then bear left on a narrow path. After an initial step down it's an easy walk back to the base of the crag.

Next: Return to the main footpath near the beck, and follow it to Wallowbarrow Farm. By the first buildings, turn right on a bridleway ('To Grassguards') and ascend this. There's a good view of the next crag early on, before the track enters the thick woods.

At the first bend after crossing the small stream, a small path goes off horizontally right. Follow this to below an obvious clean rocky prow. Bash up through bracken to reach its foot.

41: Wallowbarrow Crag: Introductory Rib 15m V. Diff

Guide Time 20 minutes

A neat, and quite intense, little route. Descent on either side is irksome, especially when the bracken is high; so the best plan is to carry, or haul, sacks up this route and go straight on up to the next one. Probably first climbed in the 1940s.

Start from the rocky platform at the base of the prow; belay on the obvious spike.

1. (15m) Step left onto the wall to the left of the prow and climb up, keeping a metre or two left of the edge. The holds are generally good, and the actual climbing is about Diff standard, but some skill and experience (and a selection of small to medium wires) is needed to find protection. Even so, it's a bold lead.

Next: from the top of the route move up and then traverse the slope leftward, to reach the right hand side of the East Buttress, which is the largest and highest section of the crag.

42: Trinity Slabs 60m V. Diff

Guide Time 1 hour 20 minutes Delete for a roped ascent

With plenty of variety, this is the best easy route - and the easiest good

Wallowbarrow Crag

route - on the main crag. Probably first climbed in 1951.

Approach: there's a short clean wall, with a big ledge at its base, near the right edge of the buttress. This is the start of Wall and Corner, officially V. Diff. However, the first pitch is a little technical and the flake which provided the best holds and only protection is now loose. Move down and left from this past a heathery break to the next clean rib of rock.

Start where a large flake leans against the base of the rock.

1. (17m) Climb the clean rib to the left of the flake until it steepens, forcing a move left. This move can be done in various ways, but none is easy or perfectly protected. Continue more easily to a large ledge and pinnacle belay.

2. (13m) Move up behind the belay to a sloping ledge, then step left onto a rib and climb it to another ledge. Step off a block and up a short wall to a large ledge. Belay on a block on the right.

3. (15m) Above the belay is an obvious groove/crack. Start off to left of this, crossing and re-crossing it before finally moving left to an oak tree belay.

4. (14m) Step up right, to another ledge, then climb shattered pillars to a small square ledge above. Move rightwards onto the wall, and make a couple of interesting moves up to easier ground and a pinnacle belay.

Descent: scramble up a few metres to a grass terrace and walk horizontally right: a narrow path appears in the heather. Follow this to the descent gully. This has a few awkward steps, so proceed with care.

And Now?
There are other routes here which the FRCC guide rates V. Diff but which we consider to be rather harder. We've already mentioned Wall and Corner. The Leaf, on the West Buttress, also has an awkward start which isn't easy to protect. At higher grades again, there are some excellent routes to be savoured - favourites being Thomas (Severe) on the West Buttress and Digitation (Mild VS) on the East.

Duddon Valley Expedition

About 370m of scrambling: up to Grade 3

The valley doesn't lend itself to a long continuous upward scramble, but has excellent routes at various levels - there's a clutch quite low down, and another on the southeast shore of Seathwaite Tarn. However the two best individual routes are the Blake Riggs, Little and Great. By approaching from the south it's easy to include Tarn Beck and then drop slightly for Little Blake Rigg. The slight plod up to Great Blake Rigg is well rewarded; it is the best, and also the hardest, route of the day.

43: Tarn Beck Grade 2 if the best line is followed, but easier alternatives can always be found. An ascent should be possible in almost any conditions.

Vertical height about 80m: guide time about 30 minutes for unroped ascent

Approach: it's a very pleasant walk from Seathwaite, or from the campsite at Turner Hall. Those with cars can save about a kilometre's walking by parking near a bend in the road below High Tongue (grid ref 231975). Drop down east and skirt a very wet area by a permissive path, then follow narrow paths through a strip of woodland. All approaches meet near a footbridge at grid ref 237977. From here the rocky spines of Crag

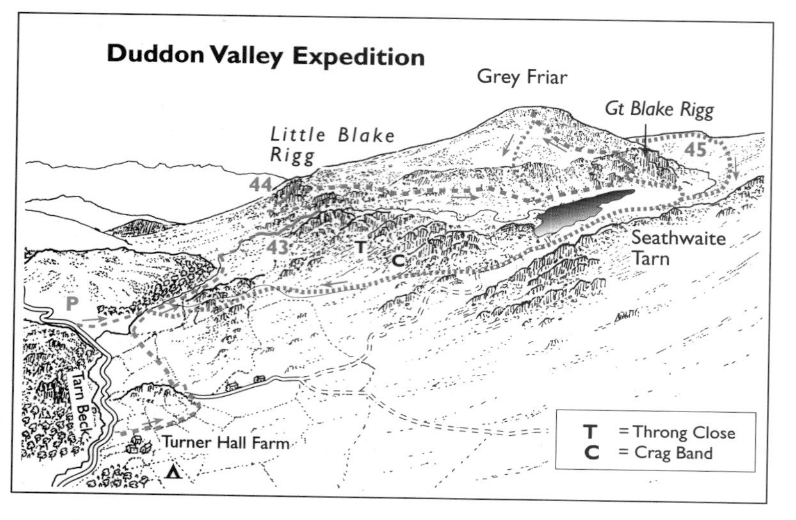

Band and Throng Close are prominent: these can also be scrambled at grades 3 and 1 respectively. However, the ascent of Tarn Beck gives the greatest variety to the day. From the footbridge head up the valley on an intermittent, and sometimes wet, path to another footbridge over the beck. Cross the bridge and go up to a clump of trees (ash and holly) between two branches of the stream. **Start** here.

Climb left of the trees past a pointed flake, then stride across a small central channel and up a sharp rib just on its right. Continue up and right to easier-angled rock. The ground above is much less steep and more broken. Unless the water flow is very low, the best general line is found by following rocks just to the right of the right-hand branch.

Where the stream concentrates into a single channel again, aim to get back into its bed, though this can be tricky if the water level is high. If you find yourself crossing a wire fence you're a bit too high up: in this case drop down left just beyond, and cross the stream by a fin of rock just above a pool.

Now go up the left side of the stream, rounding a steep rib on a narrow ledge - easier than it looks - and then up easy slabs. As the scrambling in the beck itself peters out, go left to a small steep crag and up

The flaky rib above Tarn Beck

flaky slabs, climbing over an amazing (and apparently sound) stack of flakes.

Next: You could proceed directly to Great Blake Rigg from here. However, it makes for a fuller day to head due north. In a few minutes Little Blake Rigg appears ahead.

44: Little Blake Rigg Grade 2

Vertical height about 70m: Guide time about 20 minutes for unroped ascent - once the start has been identified!

A good scramble, with lots of the excellent rock so characteristic of the valley. The rock is clean and rough and damp conditions do not make a huge difference.

Approach: about a couple of hundred metres short of the main crag, drop down the slope on the left, then traverse right (north), well above a stone wall.

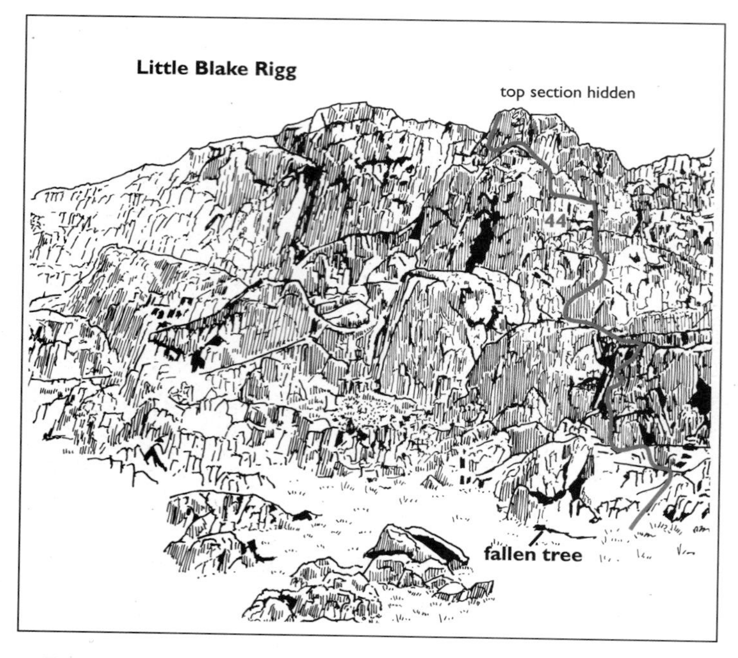

The most prominent feature of the crag is a pale wall, high up on the right, that is clearly seen when approaching from Tarn Beck. This wall is called Burnt Crag in the climbing guide (though this name appears on a quite different crag on the OS map). It's as steep as it looks: apart from one HVS at the edge, all the routes are E2 and above.

To the left of the steep wall of Burnt Crag, the main crag becomes more broken before collecting itself into several tiers of steep walls facing north-west. These are still to right of the centre of what is a very broad sprawling mass of crag. In some lights these walls can look like a collection of towers. Traverse below the crag until directly below them.

Start: almost directly below the 'towers' is a small, detached, dome-shaped buttress. The wreckage of a large tree lies at its foot, helping to confirm that you are in the right place.

Matt Lewin on Little Blake Rigg with Harter Fell in the background

The buttress itself is too steep for scrambling, so follow the much easier spine of rock to its right, or just walk around it up to the foot of the next steep nose. About 3m up this nose is an obvious block sitting on a ledge.

Climb to the block, step delicately right and climb a little groove, then continue up easier rock to a large grass shelf. Scramble up just to the right of the next steep wall, to a grassy niche below a corner. Step out horizontally left from here onto a good ledge, then climb straight up: the angle soon eases.

Another short tower lies ahead; skirt it on its left, stepping across the gully below some quartzy blocks to climb the wall just left again. This is a little delicate and the line is indefinite.

It may seem that it is all over, and far too soon, but a descending traverse to the right leads into a grassy bay funnelling down to the right. Cross its upper reaches and climb the rock beyond, to reach the foot of a grassy ramp which rises from left to right. Amble up this till it widens, then climb the rib above, with a delicate start. Beyond this there's a final flourish on the small tor which forms the summit of the crag.

Next: from here walk rightwards, trying not to lose much height, until it becomes easy to drop down onto the path along the north shore of Seathwaite Tarn.

45: Great Blake Rigg Grade 3

Vertical height about 120m: guide time about 45 minutes for unroped ascent

An impressive and serious scramble, with plenty of rock and not much grass. The rock is not as good or as clean as on the lower crags, and many people will feel the need for a rope, especially if there's even a hint of dampness. The crag is not named on some OS maps, but it is unmistakable as the large crag in several tiers above the head of Seathwaite Tarn, at grid ref 259994.

Approach: follow the path along the side of the tarn until almost below the crag. Head up steep grass, skirting to the right of an area of bouldery scree, and work across rightward to a broad terrace littered with blocks below the lowest tier of crag. Continue to the right as the terrace becomes a narrowing rake at the base of the crag. It becomes

very narrow as it sidles round a rib.

Start just past the rib, at the foot of a deep, right-facing crack. Make a couple of moves up easy ledges just right of the crack. Now you can either step left into it and make a strenuous move to reach its top, or else break out right again then step back left across the top of the crack. Either way leads to a good horizontal rock ledge. Go straight up from this on good flakes, until the rock above steepens. Sidle right on an exposed ledge to reach more broken ground above, then climb this, trending back left, to a grassy break. Follow the break up right for a few metres, then make a very steep and often wildly inelegant move to a shelf below slabs. Climb straight up these: they are uncomfortable if at all greasy.

Continue up broken rock and grass until the angle eases right off. Now walk rightwards, rising gently, to the second tier of clean rock, on the skyline.

From the lowest point of this Tier Two it's possible to climb straight up the front at about V. Diff, though it's not well-protected. The scrambling route is found by walking about 10m up left, to where the crag becomes more broken and grassy. Climb over blocks, trending leftwards at first, then gain a larger block below a steep wall. Move to the right along its top, then climb a slanting groove. Continue straight up a slabby wall on good flakes. The ground soon eases to the level crest of Tier Two.

Tier Three is a band of clean slabs over to the left. Walk across to its lowest point. There's now steep ground with some bulges directly above, so go up and left for a few metres to a cleaner slab. Climb this for about 10m, climbing over a hollow-sounding flake with care. Step left from the flake then straight up mossy-looking rock: the actual holds are quite clean. At a slight break step right and follow easier-angled but smoother rock to the top of the tier.

Tier Four is fronted by an impressive vertical wall, to the right of which is a gloomy niche. Just to the right again, a slab runs up into a slight gully. Either climb the right edge of the slab, or start in a grassy groove just to its right. From the top of the slab move up and step left across the gully to a small ledge and left again over blocks. This section feels quite exposed. Continue more easily up the crest of the tier to a grass terrace and a final steep step.

And Now?

The crag has its own summit, albeit a very minor one rising from the flank of Grey Friar. The obvious continuation is the easy walk to the summit of Grey Friar itself, with its grand view to the Scafell range. Various rocky outcrops, especially on the northern flank, tempt the scrambler to while away an hour or two. See if you can identify the cowled boulder which may give the fell its name.

The insatiable could descend from the summit via Fairfield col into the lonely valley of Tarn Head Beck. There are more possibilities here for climbers and scramblers who like exploring. Down at the southern shore of Seathwaite Tarn there are even more: Raven Nest How, Far Hill Crag, Shudderstone How and Near Hill Crag.

Dow Crag Expedition

120m scrambling, 230m climbing: up to Diff

The old spelling is 'Doe' and traditionalists pronounce it accordingly. Much of the crag is impressively steep, yet it's possible to climb the

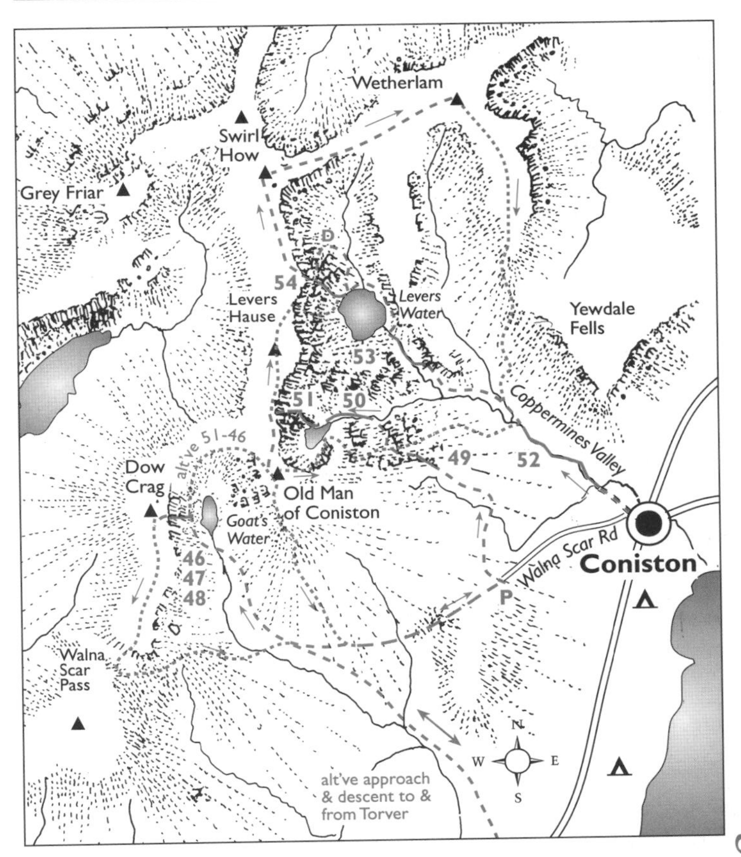

whole thing at no higher than Diff standard - and not by a flanking route either, but from bottom to top right in the middle. This is a true gift.

This itinerary gives over 300m of continuous movement (some of it downwards), nearly all on good rock. The setting high above the dark Goats Water is inspiring; on Giant's Crawl in particular, there is a powerful sense of being on a big mountain crag. The climbing never exceeds a solid Diff standard, although surrounded by much harder routes. There

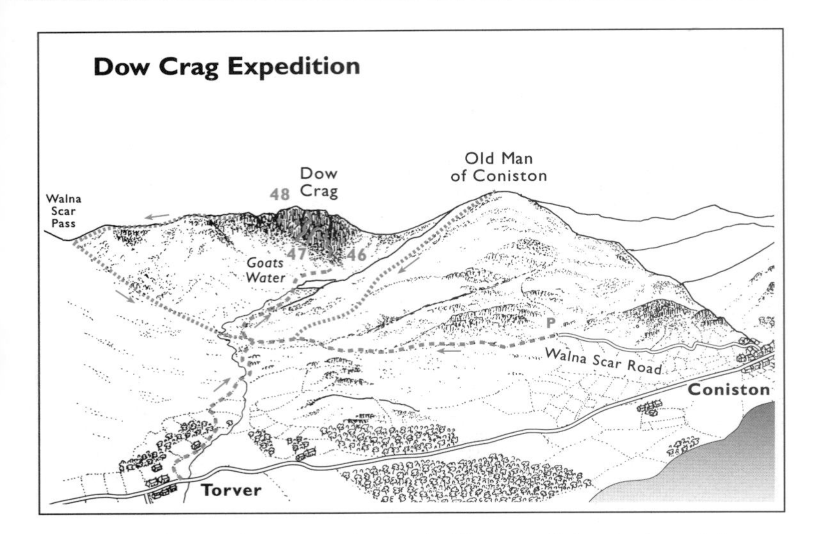

are few better days out at this grade. However, if time is short, it is possible to proceed directly to Giant's Crawl.

The rock is generally sound and rough and dries fairly quickly. The crag faces east and catches the morning sun, but the col of Goat's Hause seems to funnel winds round from the north and the crag can quickly turn chilly.

46: C Ordinary 110m Diff

Guide time about 2 hours

Easier than Giant's Crawl, and not quite matching its awesome situations, but still a fine route. The buttress is broad and open, especially lower down, and some alertness is needed to stick to the best route. First climbed in 1904.

Approach: there is no natural scrambling approach. The energetic could use the Low Water routes to Brim Fell and then drop down to Goat's Hause. Start up the ridge towards Dow until above a fringe of small crags overlooking Goats Water. Now a rough traverse, with a very

sketchy path, leads to the foot of the crag.

The usual approach is from Coniston. Those with cars can take the narrow and very steep road above the Sun Hotel, as far as the gate onto the open fell. The Walna Scar Road is followed, on foot, and then the branch path to Goats Water.

The most attractive approach, especially for the car-free, is from Torver (on the bus route between Coniston and Ulverston). A lane branches off the main road just north of the village, then a track climbs steadily past some interesting old quarries to meet the Walna Scar Road just below the Goats Water path. The crag is in view nearly all the way.

Cross the outlet of Goats Water, thread the boulder-maze, and take the right-hand route up the scree, to reach the blue stretcher box at the

Dow Crag: Climber on first pitch of C Ordinary

foot of B Buttress. Go down to the right until the path levels out below C Buttress.

Start at the lowest point of the buttress, indeed of the whole crag.

1. (33m) Climb over large flakes to the foot of a right-facing corner-crack. The crack is a bit dirty and loose in places, so step left at its foot and climb straight up the face just to its left until level with its top. Continue straight up for a few metres, on steeper rock, to more ledges with possible belays. Move left for a couple of metres, then up to easier ground. Climb a scoop, which becomes a corner, to a good ledge near the gully on the right. Nut belays in the corner above.

2. (10m) Go left along the narrowing ledge for about 3m, then climb an obvious groove to a stance on its right.

3. (25m) Move up a couple of metres directly behind the stance, then diagonally left, working out onto the open front of the buttress. Go up to a clean, exposed rock ledge with no obvious belays. Step right and make some steep moves up, with good holds and runner-spikes, to reach a pale hanging slab. A few tufts of grass, adorned with bluebells in spring, still cling to it, but the rock between them is clean. Go up the slab to a good ledge and belays.

4. (18m) Move round to the right and up a couple of metres, close to the edge of the buttress, then back left to an obvious slanting crack. This is easier than it looks, thanks to good footholds on the face. From the small ledge above, duck under a protruding block on the left and climb a short wide crack, polished by a century of struggle. Again, holds on the face help, but there's still an awkward move at the exit. A couple of metres higher is a small ledge with a belay, although if there are no problems with rope drag it is probably better to continue up the next short pitch. If you do this, place a runner at this point anyway to protect the second.

5. (7m) An obvious gangway slants up right. Climb it to a good ledge.

6. (15m) Move up again to the start of an obvious traverse line running almost horizontally back left. Follow this, with one awkward move in the

Bernie Carter on the first pitch of Giant's Crawl

middle, and from its end move up easy ground to large ledges.

47: Easy Terrace (descent) Grade 3

Vertical height about 75m: guide time about 15 minutes for unroped descent

This is the usual descent after routes on the lower section of B Buttress and other routes further right, and is usually well-populated with unroped climbers. However there are a couple of steep sections and it's perfectly reasonable to stay roped. The lower part of the descent is a rocky gully, kept clean by traffic, which gives pleasant scrambling.

Start from the top of the previous route.
Follow a level grassy path to the left. This starts to descend and becomes more rocky as it passes below the steep walls of upper B Buttress. Follow the well-trodden line down towards an obvious slanting gully. The upper section of this is narrow and chimney-like. Don't descend straight into the chimney but stay on ledges and steps just to its left for another 10m or so, before making steep moves on well-worn rock down into the gully bed. Descend this, more easily, with another steeper step near the bottom.

The steep wall above the gully has several hard climbs - there are E1's to either side but nothing easier than E4 up the central section. And our next route climbs just above it!

Next: As the gully opens out, turn right, up broken ledges and scree. Stop just before the mouth of Great Gully, beyond which rises the steep tower of A Buttress.

48: Giant's Crawl 120m Diff

Guide Time 2 1/2 hours

Giant's Crawl combines lots of good climbing, at a consistent standard, with a big-route ambience. Let's not beat about the bush: this is the best Diff in England. (Though Corvus and the New West both have their devotees - do them all and make up your own mind). The pitches as described are quite long, but there are opportunities to split them, and this is a good idea if there is nervousness in the party. First climbed in 1909.

Approach from the previous route as already described. If omitting that route, come directly from the stretcher box, following rough paths up and to the left below the walls of lower B Buttress. The huge chasm of Great Gully, with A Buttress to its left, is unmistakable.

Start: The route starts in the jaws of Great Gully (itself a worthy route of the same grade). A broad, quartz-streaked slab runs up diagonally to the right, narrowing to a gangway which vanishes from sight 'on the edge of all things'.

1. (40m) Go up ledges with remnants of grass, then climb the crack bounding the quartzy slab on its left. This is quite polished and more awkward than it looks, but there's plenty of protection. The crack eases near its top, but don't omit a final runner high up, to protect the second. At its top a broad ledge runs across to the right; the best belay is at its further end.

2. (24m) Climb up the narrowing gangway, with some overlapping steps that provide the main interest. There are steep walls above and below, creating a real sense of isolation. Finally the wall above relents and the gangway levels off. Belay with care - there are one or two unsound blocks.

3. (20m) Move right a metre or two then go up to a traverse line leading back left below more bulging rock. Protection is mostly from slings on flakes. The traverse leads to a crack formed by a block on the skyline. Make sure there's a good runner before throwing yourself at this. It is possible to climb it with some finesse but it frequently degenerates into an all-out thrutch: the secret is not to get too deeply into the crack. Once on top of the block, belay at the first opportunity. This minimises rope-drag and ensures good communication - and lets you savour your second's struggles.

4. (15m) Step left and down to a small, magnificently isolated rock ledge. It's a shame not to belay here, but it would be a 3m pitch! Above is a shallow chimney partly filled by some well-wedged flakes. Climb up this, keeping to the right side, and on up the easy groove and steps above.

5. (20m) Keep straight ahead on easier rock to the level crest of B Buttress. There is no better place to open the champagne.

And Now?

The crest of B Buttress is a privileged place, rarely visited by walkers, though in fact only easy shelving rock separates it from the busy path on the main ridge of the mountain. From here it's just a short walk, with some easy scrambling at the end, to Dow Crag summit.

If the west face were even half as imposing as the east this would be the finest peak in England, but as it is there's only a fringe of rocks above the broad moors that run down to the Duddon Valley. Still, the upper tiers are satisfyingly bare and the summit itself is a fine perch. There's a grand view full of contrast. Northwards all is fellside, rock, and scree, while to the south everything falls away to the gentle, rolling fields, woods and low moors around Coniston Water, with Morecambe Bay beyond.

From here you can descend south over Buck Pike and Brown Pike to the Walna Scar track, or north, swinging east, to descend from Goats Hause. Or, if time and energy remain, go up to Coniston Old Man and then descend its south ridge. There's scarcely a path on this and there are many scattered outcrops, but in good visibility all difficulties are easily circumvented or scrambled down.

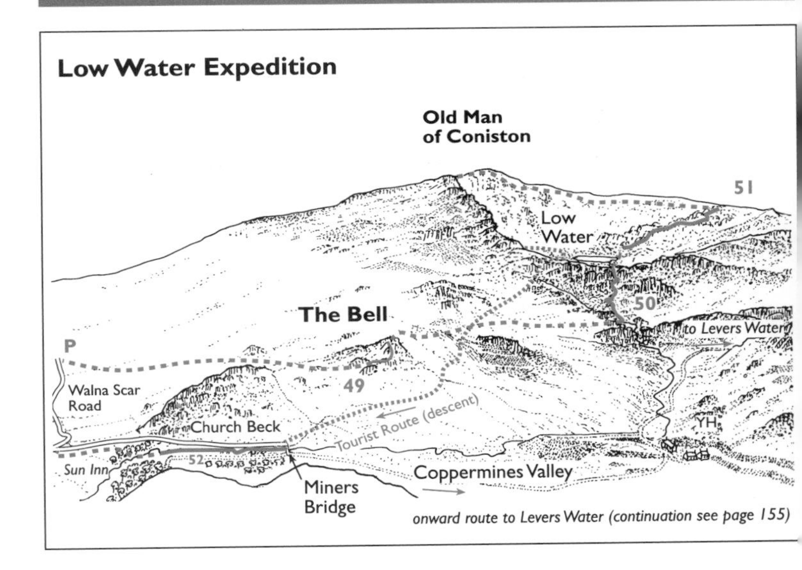

Low Water Expedition

350m scrambling, up to Grade 3

Mine and quarry workings scar the fellsides almost to the ridge-crests, though this is something you'll mostly notice on the walking sections. Most of that walking is fairly level: the height is gained by scrambling, exploiting the wealth of unsullied natural rock that remains. Busy paths are close at hand, yet you'll still feel pretty lonely as you immerse yourself in the subtleties of Low Water Beck and the complex route-finding of Brim Fell.

49: The Bell Grade 1

Vertical height about 60m: guide time about 15 minutes

This jolly little scramble makes for a light-hearted warm-up before the sterner stuff. It is easily included when you approach from the Walna

Scar Road; the walk from the fell gate takes barely 15 minutes and the climb no longer.

Approach: for those with their own transport, the easiest way is to drive up to the fell gate on the Walna Scar Road. Park just beyond the gate - driving further up the track is frowned upon and gains us nothing anyway. Those without transport will find it a dull slog up the Walna Scar Road to the gate, but there's no other convenient approach to The Bell from Coniston. Some of the tarmac can be avoided by seeking out a small path on the left-hand side of the stream.

It's also possible to approach from Torver (see Dow Crag above). This seems roundabout at the start but makes for a great descent at the end of the day, over Coniston Old Man and down the south ridge. Above the flooded quarry, look for tracks bearing right across the almost level moor, to join the Walna Scar Road. Go right, descending a little, to the fell gate.

From the car park on the Walna Scar road, take the track running roughly northward (to the right as you come through the gate). After the first bend it crosses a small beck. Go down beside this, then follow

a clear green track left (northward) to a ruin. The Bell is seen directly ahead as a miniature rocky peak. Continue along the wall then up through bracken to the base of the main rib of the crag.

Start at the lowest point of the rocks. Climb directly up the first low buttress. Walk left to the top of a sharp rib (this could be climbed from its foot, but is harder) then left again to a ledge alongside a fine slab. Go up the right-hand edge of this slab, then a V-groove directly above. Step left below a juniper and up to a more broken section.

Twenty metres higher, the rock gathers itself again. Climb direct up a clean slab with a thin crack, and straight on up a steeper step to a break. Move 3m right, to a spiky edge, and climb up this, with an awkward move past a small juniper. Now climb more broken rocks to a steepening; there's a large holly on the right and a bay just to its left. Climb the back of the bay, or the ledges just left of the holly, till the bay starts to open out, then traverse left across an exposed slab to its edge, and follow that edge up.

Keep left to find one last step and then it's all over bar some attractive slabs leading to a false summit. These you can almost walk up.

Next: the true summit is mostly grass but it's a fine spot to weigh up the prospects. A direct descent west is a bit steep and blind, so it's easier to start by walking 50m north (towards Coppermines Youth Hostel). Now go left (west) over a broad rocky rise, or follow a sheep-trod on its right flank, to a junction of tracks.

50: Low Water Beck Grade 3

Vertical height about 120m: guide time about 45 minutes for unroped ascent

Despite its name, Low Water Beck is not really a gill scramble: the most serious sections (and they are serious) are on orthodox ribs and buttresses. Unlike some gills, there's no need to wait for a drought, though it does get uncomfortable when the beck is in full spate.

Approach either by The Bell or simply stay on the track to reach the junction mentioned above (grid ref 285981). This can also be reached directly from Coniston: climb alongside Church Beck or even in it (see below) to Miners' Bridge, from where a path rises left (west) to the

track junction.
From this junction take the uphill track. Just above, round the next bend, take a branch rising gently to the right. Dwindling to a path, it leads in about 10 minutes to an unmistakable huge boulder, the Pudding Stone. This can be climbed by the slabby scoop on the south side as well as many harder routes.

Cross the combe, skirting to the left of the boggy floor and up to the gates of the cascade.

Start where the crags enclose the first fall. Climb up a tapering rib to right of the narrow channel - if the water's over the rib, consider going elsewhere! You're now directly below and possibly in the spray of the main fall. That fall is impressive but daunting. It is climbable in a drought, at about Severe, but is much more sought-after in winter. When well-frozen it's an excellent Grade III.

However, this is all academic and we need another route. This is provided by a groove in the right wall, unsuspected until you reach it. The rock needs a little care. From the platform at the top of the groove, walk about 50m up a vegetated rake, with a faint path. We want not the first break in the rock on the left, but the second, about 20m before a rowan tree. Scramble up the break to a grass ledge in a recess. As the next section is quite serious this might be the place to look for a belay.

The Pudding Stone

Go out left by a slanting crack. Use this for the feet as there are holds in the slab above. The worst bit is a long stride left onto crumbling heather ledges at the end. Move up and left again to a rib close above the waterfall. Climb the rib: the holds and the rock are generally good but the ground is steep and exposed. At its top, below a heather cornice, stride left onto a wedged boulder with a cosy recess just above.

Now go up and left on slabs usually washed by the beck, then back right on steeper rock with a splashy start. The angle eases and then the stream splits: go up the rib overlooking the right branch, on marvellous rock.

An easy section follows, then a sharp steepening looms. A direct ascent would require a real drought so move about 8m left of the fall, to a break in the steep wall. Climb this and move up a few metres to above a juniper, then slant up to the right, to the upper reaches of a slabby rib overlooking the stream. (The very bold can move horizontally

Bernie Carter on Low Water Beck

right and climb the rib in its entirety on faith and friction). There's one final fall above; it's best to climb pale slaty rock a few metres to its left.

Next: 5 minutes easy walking leads to the outflow of Low Water.

51: Brim Fell from Low Water Grade 2

Vertical height about 170m: guide time about 45 minutes for unroped ascent

Brim Fell is less serious, though you need a nose for the best line. It makes a fine conclusion, high above the copper-blue water of the tarn. The rock is generally rough and remains fairly grippy even when wet.

Approach: behind the tarn on the left, broken crags and quarry workings lead up to the summit of Coniston Old Man. At the back of the combe is Low Water Crag, all steep walls and ribs. To right of this is a more broken two-tier crag, and then a small beck. We'll climb the sprawling rocky face just right of the beck.

Walk round the tarn and then up grass and scree to where the channel of the beck is more defined. The truly incurable may find the odd bit of greasy boulder-hopping in the channel but, more to the point, the prospects for real scrambling now look bright, with a diamond of grey slabs a short way above.

Start just to right of the beck, where broken rock runs up towards the right edge of the diamond slab. Climb this broken rock until level with the slab, then go left to its foot. Climb up the slab to a slanting ledge at 4m, and continue more or less straight up, with excellent holds continually coming to hand.

After about 30m the slabs ease. Keep left for the most continuous rock, and climb the left-hand side of a steeper step. A couple more little orphaned bands of steep rock enliven the otherwise easy ascent to a distinct grassy break.

There's another lobe of slabs above, slightly undercut at its base, but you can get onto it at its bottom right corner. The rock is a little shattered here, but soon improves. Move left to a small rock ledge in the centre of the slab, then straight up.

Above the slab the rock rises in three steps. There's no real difficulty but it is more shattered. Then a bigger, steeper step bars the way. There is a possible line - at least V. Diff - up its centre, but the better part of valour is on the left. Go up a shallow gully for 5m, then back right on good slabby rock. Above this there's one last step and then, suddenly, no more rock. It's just 3 minutes stroll to the broad crest (you can hardly call it a summit) of Brim Fell.

And Now?

That may well be enough. In which case stroll easily to the summit of the Old Man. The quickest descent is by the broad, stony tourist path.

A far more elegant route is down the south ridge, although this is better avoided in thick mist. If you are hungry for more there are several possibilities:

(a) head north along the ridge to Levers Hause then down to Levers Water (see Levers Water expedition below);

(b) start south and then slope off right to Goats Hause. Climb up a little on the far side, above the first fringe of rocks, then look for a rough, narrow path leading left to Dow Crag and its airy climbs. From the Hause you can also descend rightwards to Seathwaite Tarn, where there are more scrambles (though you'll have to wade the stream to get to Great Blake Rigg).

Levers Water Expedition

160m scrambling, 70m climbing, up to V. Diff (or Diff)

Coppermines Valley was an industrial centre for centuries: the last attempt to work the copper only ended in 1935, and quarrying continued even more recently. Many of the spoil heaps remain bare of vegetation: the hills turned inside out for our inspection. Up at Levers Water, the quarrymen have left their dam and the spooky cleft of Simon's Nick. Only Great How seems to have escaped their attentions.

52: Church Beck: Lower section Grade 1, Upper section Grade 2

Lower section vertical height about 40m: guide time about 20 minutes for unroped ascent Upper section vertical height about 50m: guide time about 20 minutes for unroped ascent

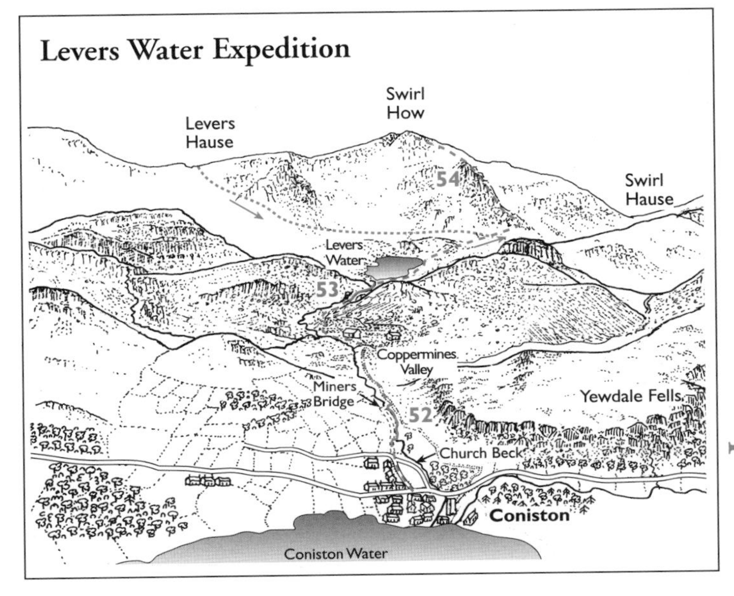

Church BeckWaterfalls near Miners Bridge

One of the most accessible of scrambles, the start is barely five minutes walk from the Sun Inn in Coniston village. This is one reason why it is so popular with outdoor centres and youth groups - the other reason is that it's great fun!

It can become much more difficult when there's a lot of water coming down, but this should be obvious well before the point where it becomes tricky to escape. Under almost any conditions there is some paddling involved.

Approach: follow the track past Dixon Ground and across the first field. Where it dips to cross a small side stream, go down right, to a bridge (grid ref 297977).

Start from the bridge. If it's possible to pass under it without getting your feet wet, there's a sporting chance of completing the trip. It's easy at first, mostly rocky walking, until an overhead pipe appears just before a weir. Bypass the weir by a channel 10m to its left. Just above is the first ravine section, which becomes particularly gloomy where it's spanned by a large dead tree; paddling is now probably obligatory.

Climb easy slabs to left of a fall to reach a more open ravine. Another large dead tree heralds more pools. Pass the first one by ledges on the left. Then there's a shallow pool and after it a deeper one. The fall at the back of this is split by a large boulder. Climbing this would be wet and desperate, except perhaps in extreme drought. So backtrack and escape up the left wall (facing upstream) on an eroded route where tree-roots are useful, to end the first section.

A bracken path runs between the beck and the main track above. Where the bracken ends slant back down across grass towards the beck.

Upper section

There are some awkward steps back down to the beck, and tree-roots are again very useful. Just above now is a fine fall below the picturesque Miners' Bridge. Paddle to the rocks just to left of the fall and climb them, working left onto slabs. Keep moving up and left, with a couple of delicate moves, to sculpted rocks above.

The bed of the beck above is coated with green algae and very slippery in many places. Paddle under Miners' Bridge, or traverse one of its walls. There's a long easy section before the walls close in again. The next real obstacle is a long pool below a fall. As the pool deepens uncomfortably, get onto slabs on the right. The lower part of the slab is normally very slippery: this makes the first moves distinctly interesting, with the prospect of a serious dunking. Holds and adhesion soon improve and you can move easily left, to arrive above the fall.

The next fall is distinctly unfriendly so traverse the right wall, carefully, via a small birch tree. Return to the bed of the beck and work round to the right of the water below a retaining wall, then up clean pale slabs to the remains of a sluice. Coppermines Valley now opens out ahead.

Next: follow the wide track to right of the stream. Coppermines Valley is almost level, with several buildings at its far end. The obvious white one is the youth hostel, and just behind it there is a display of old min-

ing machinery. Take the track which goes left in front of the hostel, curving round into the lower combe of Levers Water Beck. Here take the right branch, which climbs a little before it crosses the beck.

53: Levers Water Beck Grade 1

Vertical height about 100m: guide time about 30 minutes

An obvious path climbs steeply up the slope of mine spoil scree to left of the beck, but the beck itself is a much pleasanter alternative. It's nice way to gain height, rather than a sustained scramble: difficulties can be added or avoided at will.

Start where the track crosses the beck.
Boulder-hop up the beck to the first steep cascade. This is best climbed by rocks on its left: they are a little shattered so some care is needed. The next major fall is dealt with in a similar fashion.

The third fall is a two-stage affair, with a shelf and pool below the steeper upper section. There are several ways to the shelf, but starting on the right will avoid having to go through the stream. From the shelf make an awkward first step just to right of the water. There's usually a little spray to encourage you to make these moves decisively. Now follow steep rock with good holds, keeping close to the tumbling water.

Higher up, the stream twists through a mini-ravine below a final fall. You can either traverse the right wall to escape up the fellside, or climb a groove on the left near the entrance of the ravine. Either way, Levers Water is just above.

54: Great How Crags Original Route 70m V. Diff (or Diff if pitch 2 is avoided)

Guide time about 1 1/2 hours Small 'Friend' advised for protection of the 2nd (avoidable) pitch

Although a route of comparatively modern vintage (the first recorded ascent was in 1961), this climb has all the mountaineering feel of the early pioneering routes, as it explores the main ridge via hidden walls, pinnacles and gaps. Whilst generally straightforward, care is required with rope management to minimise drag, and the second pitch is bold and intimidating for the grade - it can be circumvented, with the grade for the rest of the route being Diff. This pitch, in particular, gets substantially harder when wet.

Approach: cross the dam and follow the track along the east shore of Levers Water, passing below the small Sunlight Crag. This has a short scramble and some rock climbs. Across the tarn, Great How is now obvious as a rocky ridge rising to a distinct peak. To its left is the slight peak of Little How, from which another rocky ridge descends, with some attractive slabs at its foot. The ridge can be scrambled, while the slabs have several climbs (see 'And Now?').

Continue round the tarn and then up to the left of the screes below Great How.

Start at the bottom of the ridge, at the lowest point of the crag.

1. (17m) Climb the ridge using big holds, to a ledge. Move right from

here to pass through a window, which brings you to a stance in a trench surrounded by huge blocks.

2. (7m) For the long-legged and gymnastic it is possible to make a bold and exposed step off the tallest block to reach a big, obvious and flat hold on the steep wall above. The short and unsupple will have to climb the wall from the stance. For climbers of any dimensions, the pitch is difficult to protect with a traditional rack, but a horizontal slot will accept a small Friend. Once established on the rib above, a few easier-angled moves lead to a huge grass ledge. Walk down the ledge to take a stance at the foot of a slab.
It is possible to get onto the grass slope on the right and walk round this pitch, with the opportunity of getting a sensational photograph of anyone who may be climbing it!

3. (13m) Climb the slab to a steep crack. Climb straight up this crack for a couple of moves. Where it widens, either finish it direct with strenuous and bold climbing, or move right to a smaller crack which is ascended delicately and pleasantly; in each case reaching a ledge above.

4. (17m) A short walk leads to a large flake. Climb this and then descend behind it to a rock bridge. Belay on the bridge if rope drag is a problem. Otherwise continue up the wall above the gap for about 3m, to belay on a grass ledge.

5. (13m) Step left from the stance, continuing slightly leftwards to another ledge. Grooves above are climbed pleasantly and easily to big grass ledges.

Scramble up for a few metres until you strike a narrow but well-worn path that angles down to the left of the buttress (facing out).

And Now?

Turn right, to follow this path to the bottom of the crag. You could now investigate the routes on Little How. Sunshine Arete is a nice little route, graded Diff but with a wicked start for the grade.

Alternatively, if a return to the bottom is not required, the same path can be followed upwards. It eventually leads to the top of the crags and the main ridge path between Levers Hause and Swirl How. The best continuation fell-walk is north to Swirl How and then down steep rocky Prison Band to Swirl Hause. From there you could return to Levers Water, but an even finer conclusion is to continue over Wetherlam. Either of its southern ridges makes a fine return to Coppermines Valley, but the most fitting finish is the rocky descent of Steel Edge, followed by a saunter across Yewdale Fells.

The Coniston Fells offer a wealth of opportunities for exploratory scrambling on excellent rock.

Great Langdale

Langdale is easy to get to, but this is only part of the reason why it is the most popular of the Lakeland valleys. Its elegant curves reveal its attractions by stages. First is the bold profile of the Langdale Pikes, the most recognisable mountain outline in England; on deeper acquaintance come the twin glacial hollows of Oxendale and Mickleden at the valley head, backed by the serrated Crinkle Crags and the presiding peak of Bowfell.

And these fells deliver what they promise: a wealth of rock, most of it rough and sound, offering easy scrambles or finger-popping extreme climbs. At our range of grades we are spoilt for choice. Across the open,

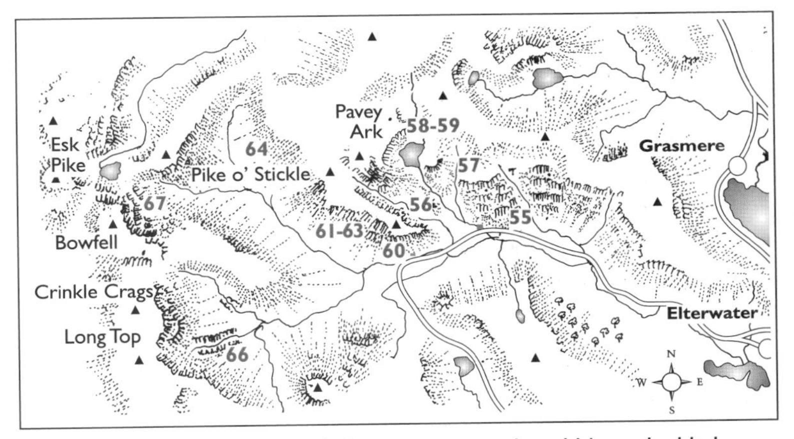

sunny face of the Pikes we include ten routes, and could have doubled that number. Despite their friendly aspect, these should not be taken frivolously. The ones on Gimmer Crag are among the hardest in this book.

Demanding, too - demanding to be climbed - is Bowfell Buttress. It has its difficulties, but above all the ambience of an inescapable route up a big buttress high on a mountain. For the competent, it is not to be missed.

Despite its obvious attractions, Langdale was a backwater in the years leading up to the First World War, with only about 20 routes recorded - though most of the climbs that we've included were among them. The period between the wars was a Golden Age of Langdale: one wonders how today's climbers would relish tackling these routes without their sticky boots and plentiful runners. The ascent of Ash Tree Slabs in 1920 was symptomatic of a growing confidence on Langdale's open, exposed faces.

Langdale climbing continued to thrive after the Second World War, especially after two of the leading climbers of the 1930s, Sid Cross and his wife Alice (née Nelson), became the licensees of the Old Dungeon Ghyll Hotel (commonly referred to as the Old DG). The Climbers' Bar - which still retains its traditional ambience - was the centre of climbing throughout the valley and beyond.

Access

Car parking in Langdale can be a real problem at busy times. The car-park at the Old DG is the best base for Bowfell and Pike o' Stickle, but fills up particularly quickly. The larger car-parks at Stickle Gill, a kilometre further east, can also be crowded out at busy periods. There is no legitimate parking anywhere else in the upper valley.

One way to avoid these frustrations is to take the bus (516 Langdale Rambler) from Ambleside, which runs as far as the Old DG. The weakness of this service is the earliness of its last bus back. On Saturdays, Sundays and Bank Holidays between late March and mid-October it leaves the Old DG at 6pm; otherwise it's around 4.30.

Amenities

There are campsites at the head of the valley near the Old DG (National Trust), and at Chapel Stile. The NT campsite has a small shop; Chapel Stile village has a shop and cafe. Hotel and B&B accommodation is plentiful but demand is also high. Information on accommodation can be found at the Chapel Stile shop and at Ambleside TIC.

There is a good choice of pubs. The Old DG has a classic climbers' bar, good ale and good-value grub, but can get very crowded. Sticklebarn is handy but lacks warmth (in every sense) while the cosier New Dungeon Ghyll Hotel (New DG) is right next door. Wainwright's Inn at Chapel Stile has a good reputation, especially for its food, but the pick of the pubs is the Britannia Inn at Elterwater.

Valley Crag: Scout Crag

55. Route 1 60m V. Diff

Guide time about 1 hour

What to do when the clouds hang low? One of the best choices for a low-level day is this fine route on excellent rock, which is rough enough to make it a reasonable proposition for a wet day. There are some exciting moments on the second pitch. First climbed in 1922.

Approach

From the top end of the Stickle Gill car-park follow the crowds past the

toilets and information point but break away to the right just above. Go slightly down below a small plantation, and cross Mill Gill.

Go up the obvious path alongside a smaller stream and on reaching open fellside fork right and follow the path round right, just above a wall. Follow this through the base of a larch wood to cross another small beck (sometimes dry). This is White Gill: the right wall of the gorge, partly seen as you look up, contains many fine routes for those climbing Severe and above.

For Scout Crag, continue just above the wall, to pass below a very steep little crag. This is Middle Scout Crag, with routes in the Extreme grades. Upper Scout Crag is just beyond, at a slightly higher level (speaking topographically: the climbing is much easier!)

Start: in the centre of the crag is a large recess with holly and ash trees. Below the recess a substantial juniper grows at 2m above ground level. Start below this.

Karen Robinson & Anne Rawlinson on Scout Crag Route 1

1. (15m) Climb a little gangway up to the left, then follow a groove-cum-crack back up to the right. Continue up a scoop and round the left side of a pinnacle to a block belay. This has a slightly hollow sound, so it's best to supplement it with a nut.

2. (25m) Head up over stepped rock trending right towards an arete. Make a bold two-step move right across a smooth little wall and round onto the arete, then continue directly up its exposed crest. There's good nut protection for the hardest moves low down. As the climbing eases, so runners become more sparse. A good ledge is reached, with various nut belays.

3. (20m) Climb straight up for another 10m; it's quite steep but on good holds. Continue up nice little walls and slabs to the slight dome of the crag top.

Descend to the right (facing downhill). Go down about 10m in a slight groove then cross grassy ledges and climb down a cracked slab into the gully. This gully needs a little care as there is loose scree and one or two precarious blocks.

There are several other routes of similar grade here - consult the FRCC guide - though this is undoubtedly the pick of the crop.

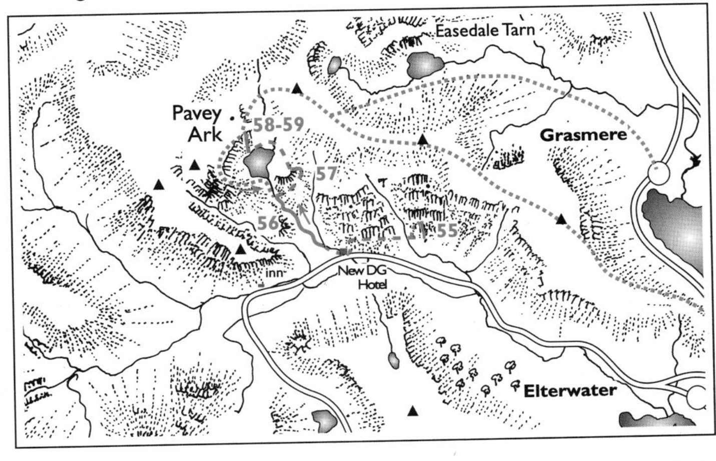

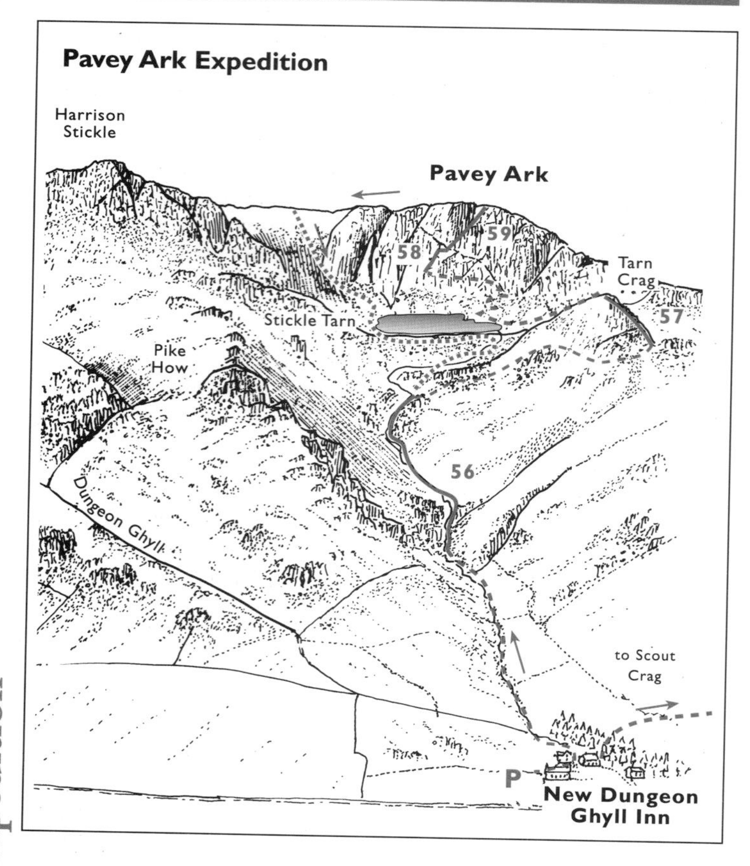

Pavey Ark Expedition

150m scrambling, 250m climbing: up to Diff

This is a great mountaineering day out, from valley to summit with a high ratio of scrambling/climbing to walking. It starts gently but builds to a climax on the fantastic upper rocks of Pavey Ark, high above Stickle Tarn. On a good day, you can do every bit of it in the sun.

56. Mill Gill Grade I

Vertical height about 100 metres, plus walking: guide time about 30 minutes

Not a major scramble in its own right but an entertaining alternative to the path. The section alongside the main cascade is reasonably continuous and enjoyable, and can easily be included in the walk up to Stickle Tarn or Tarn Crag, even if you don't follow the gill throughout. Mill Gill is the older and more correct name but it is commonly called Stickle Gill.

Approach

The obvious starting point is the Stickle Gill car park - see Langdale Introduction for more detail. From the top end of the car park walk up to left of the toilets and information point. The large path passes to left of a small plantation to reach Mill Gill.

The lower reaches of the gill can be scrambled, but unless the water is very low or you relish getting wet it's probably better just to walk up to the wooden footbridge over the gill, about ten minutes from the car-park.

Start at the footbridge. Don't cross the bridge but follow the left bank of the gill, or boulder-hop along its bed, to the first steepening. This is climbed easily enough at most states of the tide, usually just left of the stream. The best way up the next fall is by the central rib, if it's not too wet; otherwise it may have to be skirted.

A little higher there's a fine pool below a spreading yew tree. At low water it's possible to traverse round under the tree and climb to the right of the water. Otherwise back-track a bit and climb the rocks to the left; the first reasonable line lies just right of a small rowan tree, steep but on excellent holds.

Now it's easier progress to the main cascades. These sprawl across a considerable expanse of rock but it's almost always possible to climb to the right of the water, on good rock, just out of reach of the spray.

Next: Above this there's little more than boulder-hopping to the Tarn. However, just a few minutes above the top of the main cascade, an

Scrambling in Mill Gill

easy-angled rib of rock rises to the right and provides a gentle scrambling link to the base of Tarn Crag.

57. Tarn Crag East Rib Grade 2

Vertical height about 50m: guide time about 15 minutes for unroped ascent

Tarn Crag is quite extensive, but is usually bypassed by modern climbers hurrying up to Pavey Ark. In fact its rambling appearance disguises some excellent rock, with several scrambles and easy climbs. The crag also has its own distinct summit, which has a great view of Stickle Tarn and Pavey Ark. Unless you've made a very early start, this is the perfect lunch stop. Continuing the theme of gaining height without needing to unpack and repack the gear, the route described here is a fairly easy scramble, and what difficulties there are can be avoided. However if the described route is adhered to it finds a lot of excellent rough rock and very little grass.

Approach

A large central bay with several trees almost divides the crag in two, and the best climbing is to be found on the wings. There's a patch of grotty scree below the central bay and it's best to skirt below this when

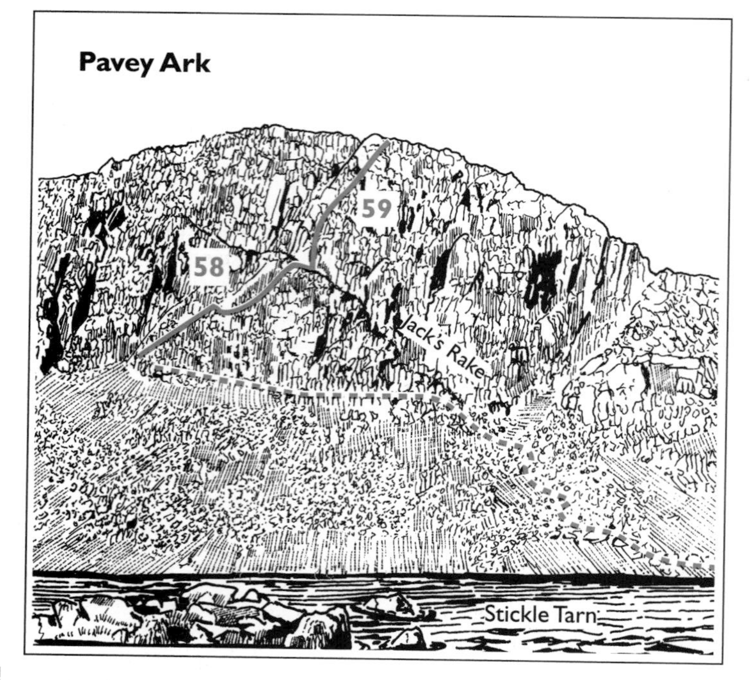

moving from one side to the other.

From Mill Gill, or from the main path, climb the easy rock rib already mentioned to reach the left side of the crag. Move right, skirt below the scree patch and pass below a rib with a small pinnacle at its base. Look for a very steep little rock wall, with a groove to its right from which a holly tree grows.

Start just right of the holly. From the lowest point of the rocks, climb the easy-angled rock to right of the holly. As the rock starts to steepen just above the holly move up to the left on excellent holds. Step left across the top of the holly-groove to a sloping platform, which feels a little exposed. From its left end move up using a large flake and continue directly upwards on easier-angled rock.

From here the best route is simply to climb straight on up, linking the best bits of rock. About half way up the crag, there's a slanting grassy break below a steep lens-shaped wall. It's tempting to attack this where it's highest and excellent starting holds sucker you in, but it's genuinely overhanging and the holds above are more rounded. Discretion is probably the better part of valour, a couple of metres to the left. Easier rocks and then walking lead to the top of the crag.

Next: fortify yourself here, and also take the opportunity to study the vast and rambling layout of Pavey Ark. The most obvious feature is the diagonal of Jack's Rake rising from right to left. There is a counter-diagonal more-or-less forming an 'X', and it is this line which our routes broadly follow.

58. Crescent Climb 98m Moderate

Guide time about 1 1/2 hours

50m rope required unless first pitch is to be split. A good supply of slings is also useful.

A mere Moderate? There's nothing 'mere' about Crescent Climb. It has all the ambience of a big mountain route. It may start innocuously, but a sense of exposure soon mounts. This reaches a climax on the traverse - the Crescent itself - which crabs a weakness between air and overhang. If your head is in order, you'll wish it was longer. First climbed in 1907.

The Crescent itself is very clean but the vegetation in the lower reaches makes the route unfriendly in the wet.

Approach

From the previous scramble, or by the busy path to Stickle Tarn. Walk round the right side of the tarn and up the eroded scree path towards the start of Jack's Rake. Cut across left below the first broken rocks, and continue along the base of the main wall. For most of its length this rises abruptly from a grassy slope, though some subsidiary rocks add interest at one point. Keep going to a pronounced break, a shallow vegetated gully, in the main wall. A prominent rowan tree grows out of the steep repellent buttress just to left of this gully, while bounding it to the right is a relatively clean, light-coloured rib of rock.

Start at the foot of this rib.

1. (47m) Climb the rib, with occasional sidesteps to left and right. You need to stay alert for protection possibilities as there are one or two tricky moves in the upper reaches of the pitch. The 50m rope will just reach to a good ledge with some old pitons in a corner (probably left by winter climbers). It's best to supplement these with a nut belay or small camming device.

The Crescent itself is now to the right and slightly higher, an obvious clean slabby break with beetling rock above.

2. (24m) Climb up a vegetated slab for a few metres until level with a small ledge at the beginning of the Crescent's clean rock traverse on the right.

You could make a tricky step directly right to the ledge. However, it's easier to move up another couple of metres; now a sling on a small spike protects the long step down to the ledge. A belay would be possible here but it's far better to continue.

The traverse itself has excellent holds, but the slab below steepens until it drops off into space and the weight of rock above accentuates the sense of exposure. Good protection is available but it is advisable to put long extenders or slings on all the runners to avoid them lifting out later - your second will thank you for this consideration! As the overhang above ends, the traverse-line reaches a ledge. Here there are good belays which give a fine view of your partners coming across.

3. (27m) Go easily straight up the narrow jug-draped slab above. Protection is available in the steep wall on the left. The most alarming bit is the transition to grass, especially if damp. Go up the grass and belay on a stout tree just below Jack's Rake.

Next: go up to the Rake, and walk about 10m to the right along a level section of path. Stop below an obvious narrow chimney.

59. Gwynne's Chimney and continuation 146m Diff

Guide time about 1 1/2 hours

This is a hearty, old-fashioned chimney climb. Approach it in the wrong

Stickle Tarn and Pavey Ark.

frame of mind and it can seem an awful struggle. But slow down, think, look around you, and it all slots into place. It is even possible to climb it elegantly. The second pitch is completely different: sunny and open. Above that there's some vegetated scrambling, but there's also a lot of lovely rock, and the finish could hardly be better. As the rock is extremely rough where it matters most, wet conditions are not a great handicap.

It is one of the earliest routes in Langdale, first climbed in 1892 by a party led by H A Gwynne, though said to have been descended earlier by Haskett-Smith.

Approach either from the previous route, or ascend Jack's Rake to the first level section

Start: the chimney, which is deep and obvious, rises above the right-hand end of the level section about half-way up Jack's Rake. (There is a much larger chimney above the start of the Rake - this is Rake End Chimney, also Diff.)

1. (20m) Climb easily into the chimney. Matters become more involved as it narrows, and rucksacks can be an encumbrance. It is occasionally necessary to have eyes in the back of your head to find all the holds.

There's a stout juniper growing from the left wall about 18m up. Diehards will continue straight up the narrower chimney above, but most people will take the opportunity to swing out right, helped by a hidden hold just round the edge. Belay in the corner just beyond.

2. (18m) Move up to the right, then slightly left up a small corner to a ledge overlooking the narrows of the chimney. Step right and climb a short groove to sudden exposure, then climb up left to a large grassy bay with good belays. The direct ascent of the entire chimney also leads to this bay.

3. (18m) Start up the vague gully-line above, moving round to right of projecting blocks and onto the rib that forms the gully's right-hand edge. Belay at an interruption of the rib line just above.

4/5. From here it's about 90m to the top, taken in two pitches. The gully line is a good guide: wherever possible climb the rocks just to its right. These develop an incredible cheese-grater texture. It's hard to slip on this stuff, but you certainly wouldn't want to! A groove in the rib and a final steep step make a satisfying finish, close to the summit.

And Now?

The obvious plan for the mountaineer is to descend Jack's Rake, though this can be a little tiresome when it's busy. Alternatively you can either head west towards Harrison Stickle and descend a path between it and Pavey to the tarn, or descend east on an eroded path into the little valley of Bright Beck. From Stickle Tarn the obvious route is straight down Mill Gill, but a pleasant alternative is to take in the scenic little peak of Pike How and finish by the steep path looping round to its right.

Those who arrived by bus can extend the day by walking from Pavey's summit to Thunacar Knott then contouring round to Sergeant Man, from where they can descend via Easedale Tarn to Grasmere. It's also possible to return to Ambleside over Blea Rigg and Loughrigg Fell. This is a surprisingly long and undulating walk, though very enjoyable, with an abrupt final descent into Ambleside.

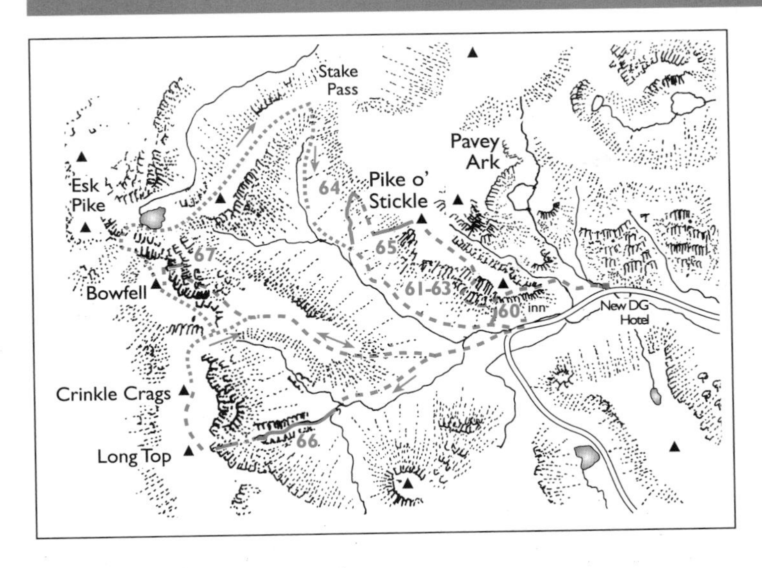

Gimmer Crag Expedition

About 100m scrambling, 244m climbing: up to V. Diff

Abseil descents are available (though not obligatory) on Gimmer: for these you will need two ropes of at least 40m (or one of 80m). Do not attempt the abseils unless you know exactly what you are doing.

Gimmer Crag was much loved in the 1920s and 1930s, when plimsoll-clad climbers began to edge away from the gullies and chimneys onto the open faces, and it has continued to delight succeeding generations. Although it isn't the biggest crag in Langdale, it has a grand situation. Gimmer is a byword for exposed climbing, on some of the best rock you'll ever find, with small but secure holds.

Despite its high mountain location, Gimmer Crag has something of an 'outcrop' atmosphere. One rarely sees parties climbing in big boots and rucksacks. The routes finish at the crag top (though the summit of Loft Crag is not far above) and descent is often made by abseil. The rock is very clean and the friction is good; wet conditions affect the grades

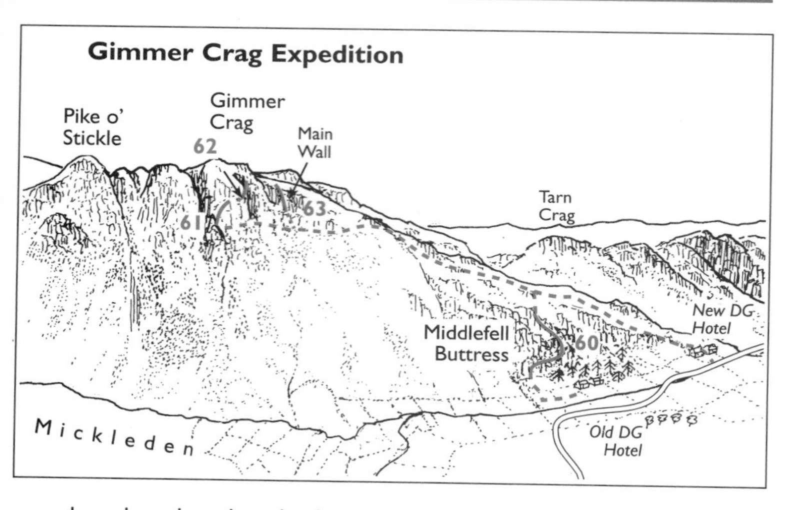

here less than they do the very polished Middlefell Buttress, and the rock dries quickly. However Gimmer provides very little shelter.

The steep slopes below, which contribute so much to the atmosphere, mean that a direct approach to the crag is a nose-down grind. Instead, start by climbing Middlefell Buttress, and follow it with some easy scrambling before a level walk leads across to Gimmer.

The best plan now is to climb Ash Tree Slabs and Oliverson's without sacks, then descend to collect them before climbing Main Wall, to continue to the summit of Loft Crag.

60. Middlefell Buttress 82m Diff

Guide time about 1 1/4 hours

Middlefell Buttress has probably given more people their first experience of rock climbing than any other route in the Lakes. But don't underestimate it! For some it turns out to be the only experience and their struggles, curses, and occasional tears remind us that this is, indeed, a real rock climb. If the clouds hide Gimmer and Pavey, Middlefell is worthwhile in its own right.

The volume of traffic means that the route is squeaky-clean, though

flanked by fine gardens of heather. However, there are some polished sloping holds which can feel very slippery in clumsy boots or when it's wet (though it does dry very quickly). All this was very different on the first ascent in 1911, by a party including Siegfried Herford, one of the most famous of early Lakeland climbers. This and neighbouring Raven Crag had previously been ignored, though there were already several routes on Gimmer; the early climbers tended to focus on the higher crags.

Approach: the obvious starting point is the Old Dungeon Ghyll Hotel. Only early starters are likely to find a parking space here, but it is the terminus of the bus service from Ambleside. Walk up right of the hotel, round behind it and through a gate, then half right to a tall stile leading into a plantation. Above this a well-built path zig-zags up to the base of the crag: ignore the right fork towards Raven Crag.

Start: The lowest tier of the crag has some obvious cracks. The central one is very steep and awkward to start, while the right-facing diagonal line is a little easier, but still probably worth Severe. For a start more in keeping with the standard of the rest of the route, begin below the deep chimney on the left side of the tier.

1. (14m) Climb the chimney and through a hole out to the left - rucksacks probably need to be removed for this. Pop out of the hole into the gully on the left of the crag. Go on up a slight step in the gully bed then back onto the rock.

Climb over blocks and round behind a leaning square-topped pinnacle, with a strenuous move over a chockstone. Step off the top of the pinnacle and make another strenuous move over a block to a ledge. It's all well protected, but beware of rope drag - for which reason it's best to belay here.

On Raven Crag photo: Ronald Turnbull

2. (4m) Climb a short step to a large terrace. It's very tempting to run this pitch together with the next, but this makes it hard to manage the rope properly.

3. (8m) The obvious scratched line up the right side of the next wall is quite steep but well protected. The ledge above has a number of blocks: the best belay is with the main rope round the biggest one.

4. (40m) There's a steep wall directly behind the blocks. Start near the right-hand side of the clean rock and move up and left for 3m via an unpleasant mantelshelf onto a ledge. Climb the obvious groove above and emerge onto a ledge on the right, about 15m up. It's possible to belay here. Above this the angle eases back. Romp up to a broad flat neck where the buttress runs back into the hillside. Belay on another large block.

Walk to the base of the next steep wall and start from its right side.

5. (16m) Climb a ramp running up to the left. Whether you start with hands or feet on this, there's an awkward move where it runs out. Swing round left into the centre of the wall then climb straight up - steep but well-protected - to a small ledge. A very smooth scoop above gives a fun finish, though it can be awkward for short people and those in clunky boots. Above is a grassy shelf, with belays a few metres back.

Next: climbing ends here, and as the next section of scrambling is long and easy, it's certainly worth coiling the rope and, if necessary, changing back into walking boots.

Go up a short step onto a grassy, rock-strewn slope. The gully separating Middlefell Buttress from Raven Crag is just to the right. A ledge leads round the head of the gully, just above a clump of ash and rowan trees, and out onto the easy upper section of Raven Crag.

NB: It is possible to descend from here, by walking across the top of the crag until above a large oak tree. Descend over blocks in its shade - awkward, polished and exposed - and go behind it to escape from the crag. This is probably worth Grade 3.

Pick a line up a succession of little steps. The easiest way is never above Grade 1; there are some damp and mossy areas but the underlying rock has good friction. As the slope becomes more broken slant up to the right onto easy slabby rock, then climb a steep little knoll just above.

Just above this, at a grassy shoulder with a cairn, you meet a walkers' path (the approach from Stickle Gill). Follow this leftward, climbing gently, soon emerging onto a broadly level shelf. Just above is the rocky front of Thorn Crag. There's a scramble up its front. This is out of our way, but the rock is so glorious it's a shame to miss it - Grade 1 by the easiest line. You could leave rucksacks at the base and scramble up and down in 20 minutes.

Otherwise keep following the main path to the left. At a large cairn just below a ruined sheepfold, where the wider path begins to climb again, a smaller one goes off to the left on a generally level course. Follow this until Gimmer's southeast face comes into view. A deep gully separates the main crag from the rock further right - which, confusingly, is called Main Wall.

If you don't plan to carry rucksacks, they are best left at the well-trodden area directly below the southeast face. From here, investigate the 30m scramble onto the end of Ash Tree Ledge - you may be descending this later on, but it's much easier to locate the route for the first time from below.

61. Ash Tree Slabs 47m V. Diff

Guide time about 1 hour

A superb route, especially the first pitch. Although the holds and protection are generally good, there's an uncompromising quality about it. It's the sort of route that's often described as 'good value' - the climbing is well sustained at the grade and the atmosphere is that of a harder route. First climbed in 1920.

Approach

The best approach is via Middlefell Buttress, as described above. If this does not appeal, a direct path skirts to the left of Middlefell Buttress, but this is a steep slog. A longer but gentler alternative starts from Stickle Gill, crossing Dungeon Ghyll and climbing the slopes above Raven Crag to the broad shelf below Thorn Crag, where it meets the route up from Middlefell Buttress.

From the trodden area below the southeast face, descend a rough

path to the toe of the broken buttress below the main crag. The path climbs again on the other side to below an obvious large corner, with a steep right wall and a sweep of clean slabs on its left.

Start: scramble up a few metres to a little nook at the base of the corner.

1. (20m) Climb up the corner for a few metres to a small spike and a nut runner. Move out left along a rising flake line, whose great handholds moderate the increasing exposure. Climb the slab above near its left edge to a small ledge. It's possible to belay here but there's a better stance just 3m higher, with a wide choice of nut belays.

2. (27m) Climb the groove directly above the stance for a few metres then move out to the right onto slightly easier slabs. Continue fairly directly upwards, and into a left-facing groove. This leads up to a large ledge and good belays below the steep upper walls.

Next: It is easy as well as sensible to stay roped for the short connection to the next route. Move to the right end of the ledge and climb down a short wall to a still larger ledge, known as Ash Tree Ledge, though it's many years since it had any ash tree.

62. Oliverson's Variation and Lyon's Crawl 60m V. Diff

Guide time about 1 1/4 hours

This is the easiest route up the open face above Ash Tree Ledge. Though the climbing is easier than on Ash Tree Slabs, it is always entertaining, and the route does find some very exposed positions. It crosses several other routes, so a certain amount of patience may be required on busy days. First climbed in 1907, though in two separate pieces.

Approach from the previous route, as described. It is also possible to scramble directly to Ash Tree Ledge from the rucksack dump below the southeast face.

Start about 3m left of the drop off at the right end of Ash Tree Ledge.

1. (10m) Climb up easily to a good ledge below steeper rock.

2. (17m) Traverse right from the ledge for about 6m then make a couple of steep moves up a slight groove and out right to a small ledge. Just to the right is an obvious corner. Climb this to sloping ledges and nut belays.

Dow Crag: Liz Bruce on the 1st pitch of Giant's Crawl

3. (15m) Follow a diagonal crack up to the right, then move horizontally right on good holds for about 4m. Move up a little on shattered-looking rock. Above is a broad groove known misleadingly as Green Chimney: it is a little green, but it's no chimney. Cross it just above its base to some obvious holds leading out across its right wall. Just round the corner is a superb ledge, the Crow's Nest. Belay here.

4. (17m) From the right end of the ledge, move up onto a slab then climb slabs and walls above. There's scope for variation, but the best climbing is generally found near the left edge. Belay where the angle eases distinctly.

Next: the abseil point, if required, is about 20m to the left, at roughly the same level: a stout chain under a hefty boulder on the edge of the crag. The abseil is 40m, so requires 80m of rope. Check there are no climbers below before throwing ropes down. The abseil leads directly back to Ash Tree Ledge near the start of Oliverson's.

From here scramble down to the right, on a series of ledges just below the steep rock, to a second abseil point where the ground steepens. There is no chain here but there are usually old slings. Inspect these carefully before you trust your life to them! This abseil leads directly back to the area where sacks were left.

It is also possible to scramble down to this point, avoiding the second abseil, but route-finding from above is tricky; easier if you reconnoitred earlier.

If abseiling does not appeal, or if you only have a single rope, then your descent is by **South-east Gully**. This descent is quite awkward and it is no disgrace to stay roped up until clear of the initial chimney. It is also a good idea to keep your helmet on, as others descending above you may dislodge stones.

Scramble up short walls above the finish of Lyon's Crawl, trending right to the steep edge of the gully. Look for a near-level platform of bare rock, quite polished near the edge, below a short steep wall.

From this lower yourself carefully into a gloomy chimney. Descend this for a few metres and then move out onto more open rock in the centre of the gully. The step out is awkward for short climbers and a sling on a handy spike is often used.

Now descend a series of steps in the middle of the gully. As it begins to open out, keep left (facing out), close to the base of Main Wall, until almost level with the sack-stashing area on the other side of the gully.

63. Main Wall 54m V. Diff

Guide time about 1 hour

A good climb to finish with, and usually less crowded than the other routes. Its unpopularity means that the route is less well-marked than the others, but this is still Gimmer, after all, so the rock remains clean and sound and the holds good. The first ascent was made in 1921, though probably not by the exact line now followed.

Approach: The descent of South-east Gully leads to the start. Otherwise, follow rough paths up towards the gully, keeping to the right side, until it closes in.

Start in the mouth of South-east Gully, roughly opposite the abrupt edge of the main crag, below the right side of a clean wall. There is a large block part-buried in the ground.

1. (19m) The first moves are probably the hardest on the route. Step off the block and move up and to the right, to get into a groove on the very edge of the wall. Follow the groove, which gets deeper, to a small ledge.

2. (35m) Move left, round onto the wall facing the gully, and climb diagonally up left to the right end of a long narrow ledge. Go up and slightly right to another small ledge (a possible stance). Move up left, in a broad shallow scoop, above which the climbing begins to ease. Belay on good ledges where the crag begins to break up into smaller steps.

And Now?

It may be worth staying roped for the initial scrambling above, until the angle eases right off. Keep on scrambling up by easy rock ribs. The summit of Loft Crag is almost directly above, while off to the right, across the upper reaches of a shallow gully, is an obvious small 'bonus' crag of very clean rock with several striking grooves and cracks. This is unsuspected by 99% of climbers on Gimmer and to do a route or two here gives a little flavour of pioneering.

From the summit of Loft Crag, drop down the short back side and follow the path rightwards. Descend a steep, repaired section between Loft Crag and Thorn Crag to return to the shelf below the latter (and another opportunity to frisk about on its amiable rock). The path leads down, beside the gorge of Dungeon Ghyll, reaching the valley near Stickle Gill.

Pike o' Stickle Expedition

360m scrambling and climbing: up to Moderate

If you don't think it's possible to escape the crowds in Langdale, try this trip. The two routes both take you away from the busy paths, yet in every other respect they could hardly be more different. Troughton Beck offers comfortable seclusion, while on Pike o' Stickle the loneliness is of a starker sort. You feel the exposure and seriousness even before you start moving upward, and more so on the upper rock steps. There are plenty of harder routes in this book, but few which feel so committing.

64. Troughton Beck Grade 1

Vertical height about 120m: allow up to an hour for unroped ascent, not because of any difficulty but to appreciate the beauty of the beck

Troughton Beck is a hidden gem of a place. It may tempt you to linger, especially with the foreknowledge that Pike o' Stickle is made of altogether sterner stuff. There isn't a great deal of scrambling, but what there is is very pleasant and the surroundings are delightful.

Approach

Start from the Old Dungeon Ghyll Hotel; from just above it, follow the near-level track into the great glacial hollow of Mickleden. The path sweeps along below Gimmer Crag and Pike o' Stickle. There's an open and fairly straight section of track before reaching the first of the moraine mounds near the head of the valley. Troughton Beck is the first significant watercourse west of Pike o' Stickle, with a bouldery debris fan lower down. It's about 30 - 35 minutes walking from the hotel.

Start: go up the right side of the fan, with only faint sheep tracks. Above

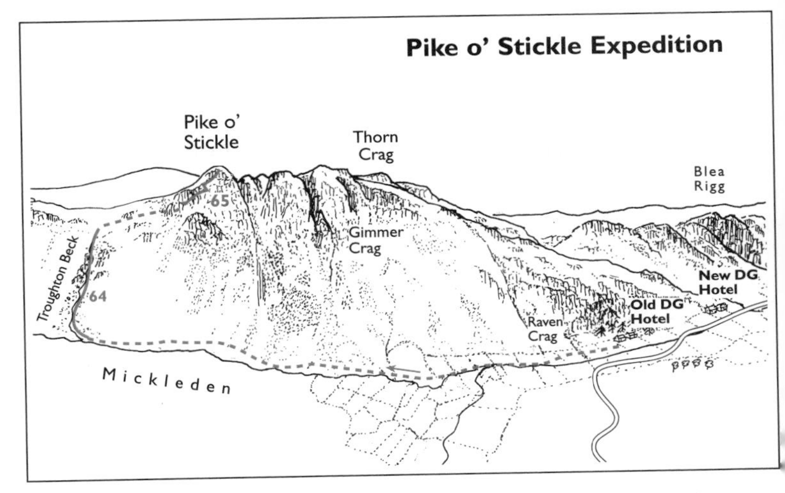

this the beck flows in a well-defined little valley. Uphill walking shades into mild scrambling as the valley closes in.

Detailed description is unnecessary: follow the beck. Much of the ascent is boulder-hopping, interspersed with short rock steps. The rock varies from a slate-blue to magenta in colour, and the sides of the gill are decorated with foxgloves, parsley-fern, bilberry and heather.

High up there's a step, larger than most of the preceding ones, where the rock is distinctly more shattered. Above this the angle eases back into an almost level trough. There's a sort of fork, with steep scree in the right branch. Climb - with care - up an earthy line left of the water-fall in the left branch. As the valley opens out a little just above, exit rightwards on steep grass.

65. Pike o' Stickle South Face Grade 2 scrambling at first, then Moderate climbing

Vertical height about 240 metres: allow two hours

Scrambling? Climbing? The word for this is mountaineering: an Alpine grade (about PD) would be as appropriate as anything. Looking at the route in more detail, there's a long preamble of vegetated scrambling. It's not difficult and most people will be happy to move unroped, but there's a strong sense that it would not be a good idea to slip. Once you reach the clean rock of the upper cone, it's time to rope up. Those who are competent in Alpine technique will be able to move together for most of the way. Otherwise, take belays and place runners where possible. Four or five slings and a few medium to large nuts (such as 6, 7, 8, 9 Rocks) should suffice. Well-equipped parties able to operate comfortably at V. Diff standard will find much scope for direct variations. Although the upper rocks are clean, the lower scrambling section will feel doubly insecure in damp conditions.

Approach: from the top of Troughton Gill, keep trending right and slightly up, past small outcrops and scatterings of boulders. The slope eases, but there's no need to go all the way up to the level crest of the moor. Instead contour round towards Pike o' Stickle, now an obvious cone straight ahead.

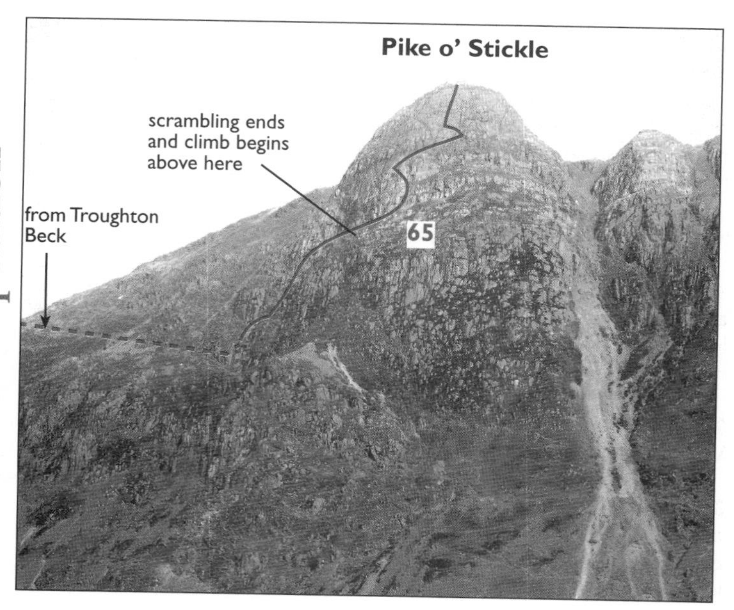

Approach a little closer and a complete profile of the Pike can be seen, rising from a long sweep of scree. It can be roughly divided into three sections: the upper cone of bare rock, a more broken middle section, and then steep vegetated crags below. Between the middle and lower sections there's a grassy shoulder, and this is the place to aim for. Cross the steep hillside with care, then cross the scree-run with even more care to reach the fairly flat shoulder.

It is also possible to reach this point directly by a mindless slog up alongside the scree-run, but Troughton Beck is infinitely nicer.

Start from the shoulder that forms the foot of the broken middle section of the face.

Continue round to the right; there are faint traces of path, descending slightly. A 10m prow of vertical rock appears ahead and just beyond it you can see a gully splitting the lower crags. Go up the broken slope to left of the prow until it becomes rocky above; then contour to the right, just above the prow, into the upper reaches of the gully.

Walk and scramble up the gully for about 20m, until it is almost blocked by a steep rock slab. Outflank this on its left then move back right above it on traces of a path. Go up right to a more open grassy slope. The more continuous rock of the upper cone is now seen above. Follow the slope up and right, with more traces of path, towards the right-hand edge of the lowest tier of steep clean rock.

On the corner of this tier there's an obvious block with an overhang at its base. Just below it is a good place to rope up.

1. (25m) Go up right towards the base of the block, then back left on an obvious ramp, with at its end an awkward move onto a projecting ledge. Step left and up to grass. Choose any route up the next band of rock - several are possible - to another grassy break below a steep wall.

2. (20m) The wall has a recess with an overhang above its right side. Walk up and right, to the point directly below the recess.

3. (20m) Go up stepped rock, working left to a ledge roughly level with the overhang. From a spike at its left end make a steep move up then climb straight up, with the angle gradually easing, to belays on more broken rock.

4. (50m) Walk up to a table-like block just below a steep band of compact grey rock. Walk to the right below this face for about 20m, and climb an awkward step formed by some stacked blocks. Continue up steeper broken ground and ascend a kind of trench. There are poor belays above it.

5. (25m) Move horizontally left past an excellent spike runner to the apparent edge of the buttress. From here go up diagonally left to a large block on a terrace. There are good belays just to left of the block.

6. (35m) Directly above the large block is a shallow groove. Climb up this, taking to the right-hand wall where necessary. As the groove fades out, continue straight up easier slabs. Good, though small, belays are eventually found.

From here less than a rope-length of ever-easier ground leads to the summit, where there's usually a surprised audience.

And Now?
At the back of the summit cone, drop easily to the level ground behind. The easiest way down, and probably the best for avoiding the crowds, is over Martcrag Moor to the Stake Pass path and so down into Mickleden. However, a descent by the path alongside the upper ravine of Dungeon Ghyll gives access to a choice of scrambles on Harrison Stickle.

Bowfell Expedition

350m scrambling and boulder-hopping, 108m climbing, up to V. Diff

There is no more aptly-named fell in Lakeland than Crinkle Crags. The skyline dips at Three Tarns and then rises to the commanding peak of Bowfell. There is a lot of rock high on these slopes, much of it forming magnificent crags. The jewel in the crown is Bowfell Buttress: one of the best rock-climbs in England at any grade.

The climb is amply worth the effort of its long and steep approach walk, or of the rather roundabout scramble described here. Either approach does provide an incentive to travel light. A spring below

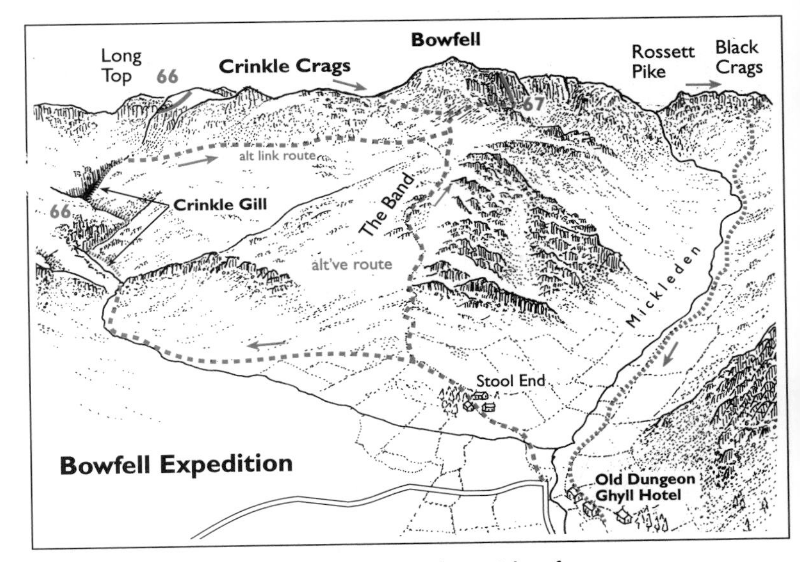

Cambridge Crags allows you to save on the weight of water.

66. Crinkle Gill and Crinkle Crags Grade 1

Vertical height of scrambling about 350 metres: allow two hours

A good alternative to the trudge up The Band, especially on a hot day, is to follow one of the gills running down into Oxendale. Crinkle Gill is probably the best of these. There's only a little scrambling, but some impressive rock scenery. Above the gill, it's possible to make a long rightwards traverse across rough slopes to get to Bowfell Buttress, but it's more fun, and not a lot more effort, to scramble on up to the ridge of Crinkle Crags.

Approach

Just past the Old DG the road takes a sharp left but a farm track continues straight ahead across level fields to Stool End Farm. Once through the farmyard, the way divides; the path onto The Band rises to the right,

Scrambling in Crinkle Gill: the little rock channel
photo Ronald Turnbull

but take the route on the left into Oxendale.

The Oxendale approach runs almost level to the head of the valley. Don't cross the first footbridge on the left but keep straight on to a second. This crosses the lower reaches of Hell Gill: Crinkle Gill is the next stream on the left.

It is a very easy scramble which hardly needs detailed description. Follow the gill! After the first pools, the main stream line appears to run directly up the slope but this is in fact a side-stream dead end, and you turn left into a little rock channel. This gives a nice little bit of rock work. Above this there's a long scenic walk, with odd bits of boulder-hopping, between rock walls. Several of these have been developed to give a series of Extreme routes, though you will rarely see anyone on them. Finally the stream splits into several small branches, with the best way being on the clean rock under the tiny waterfall of the left hand branch.

Now you emerge onto open slopes. It is possible to walk right from here: pass above or below the easy-angled outcrop of Low Bleaberry Knott and then keep below all further crags until you can rise slightly to the level shoulder at the top of The Band. This traverse proves quite tedious and unless you really can't put Bowfell Buttress off any longer, it's better to head on upwards for some easy buttress scrambling.

A pale swathe of scree drops from a gap in the rocky skyline: this is Mickle Door. We'll climb the easy-angled buttress to right of this scree. Slant up north, passing a boulder cave, to the foot of the buttress. From the bottom right corner, go up a few feet and traverse left on rocky ledges towards a little gully. The easy way up the first tier is in this gully: you can also climb steep and rather exposed rock (Grade 2) with good holds on the right of the gully.

From the top of the first tier, head first left then back right on grassy ledges: or more directly upwards on rock (Grade 1). At the skyline crest turn up left to a cairned top (Gunson Knott).

Next: Only 50m away southwest is Long Top, which is the high point of Crinkle Crags, so it may as well be visited. Then head north on a well-used path across the many tops of Crinkle Crags, eventually dropping to the major col of the Three Tarns.

Ignoring the wide path ahead, take the cairned path down right towards the Band and Langdale. After 200m contour to the left below a line of screes to reach the crest of Bowfell's east ridge. Here turn uphill on a small path. The path becomes pitched for 100m, then turns right and contours off northwards. This contour-path is known as the Climbers' Traverse.

67. Bowfell Buttress 108m V. Diff

Guide time about 2 hours

This is about as good as it gets. Bowfell Buttress has it all: an elegant line, a commanding position, a mountain-top finish, excellent rock, diverse and absorbing pitches and comfortable stances. And no, it would not be better if it were nearer the road.

However, it must be said that this is the hardest route in this book. Crucial holds have become highly polished over the century since the first ascent, and if the route were not so steeped in tradition it might

Bowfell
Buttress
67
normal
finish
suggested
alternative
finish
route here
is slightly
hidden -

already have been upgraded to Mild Severe. Still, it's too good to leave out!

Be aware, then, that this is a challenging route, even in perfect conditions, and it can become much, much harder when damp. The slimmed-down 'classic' rack which many people carry on low-graded climbs may be inadequate: most will be glad of a few smaller wires to protect the crux crack. And it is by no means unknown for these to be used for direct aid!

First climbed in 1902. Thank you, T Shaw, G H Craig, G R West, C Hargreaves and L J Oppenheimer.

Approach

Either from the previous route, or slog up the Band until it eventually levels out. While the main path slants away leftwards towards to the col of Three Tarns, a branch on the right heads more directly uphill, aiming for a rocky ridge dropping from the summit of Bowfell. As the path winds up the steepest part of this ridge, there's usually a cairn to mark the divergence, rightwards, of the Climbers' Traverse.

This well-defined and generally level path runs below Flat Crags and Cambridge Crags, and it is well worth knowing that there is a spring at the very foot of the latter. Clear and cold, it has never been known to dry up. The path contours on across a broad scree apron. Bowfell Buttress lies at the far side of this. The direct approach takes about an hour and a half, that by Crinkle Gill probably an hour longer, in neither case allowing for rehydration time at the spring.

Start at the left side of the base of the buttress. A long straight gully/chimney hangs above.

1. (22m) Climb broken rocks to just below the gully/chimney (possible stance and belay for those who need encouragement on the next bit). On the right is a short chimney, obvious by its high gloss. It is all too easy to start flailing around and add to the polish. High holds on the right rib aid the determined pull out onto a good ledge. Shorter climbers may consider this to be the crux pitch.

2. (32m) Climb the wall behind the ledge on good holds, moving left after 12m to a possible stance and belay. Continue up the shallow chimney above, or the rib on its right; this rib is well-endowed with spikes.

Easy ledges lead to a substantial balcony, still quite grassy. Walk to the right to the bottom of an obvious crack in the steep little wall.

3. (16m) For most people this is the crux. The crack is just a bit too long to feel like a boulder problem, despite the good landing. It's steep, and the holds are polished and small. A decisive approach pays dividends, but the pull-out is onto slabby rock rather than a flat ledge. Traverse left, below another steep wall, to a large spike belay.

4. (18m) Traverse left on a narrowing band of slabs then climb a groove which becomes more of a chimney. Move up and left again, across a fairly steep wall, to reach a welcoming ledge.

5. (20m) Climb the deep groove above until it splits. The usual finish is by the left branch, but the fine hanging slab on the right is even better. Scramble (still roped) up the final little steps to the crest of the buttress.

And Now?

Walk along the neck between the crag and the main ridge of Bowfell, then left and up boulder-strewn slopes to the summit. It may not be the best mountain summit in the Lakes, but it has the best mountain view. It is good in all directions, but best of all westwards over the hollows of Lingcove Beck and upper Eskdale to the Scafell ridge. Lush pastures in lower Eskdale glow softly green, in utter contrast to the bony, bouldery ridges.

The obvious route down is to follow the well-worn descent path, or pleasant easy slab scrambling to its left (facing downhill), to Three Tarns and then back down the Band in around an hour. But there are better routes, unless time or energy are low.

If you've been over Crinkle Crags on the way up, why not walk north over Bowfell and down to Ore Gap, then down by chilly Angle Tarn, over Rossett Pike and down by Stake Pass. If you came up The Band, now is the time to savour the intricate ridge of Crinkle Crags. By now it will probably be late afternoon and the crowds that swarm along it in the middle of the day will mostly have gone. Scramblers will enjoy straightening out some of the kinks of the path, but be wary on descending sections. There are no major crags but many short steep walls lurking. Either alternative will take 2 hours or more from Bowfell summit.

What to do when it's raining

A: Go climbing

All the routes in this book, and some much harder ones, can be and have been climbed in the rain. Most of them have also been ascended in full winter ice cover! However climbing in the wet can be disconcerting. You may be fairly experienced on dry rock, but climbing when it's wet or cold sends you back almost to square one.

The best routes for this are those where the rock is clean and rough - the ones that would be in the sun if only it wasn't raining! Many of the routes on the Langdale Pikes fall into this category, as do those on Grey Crag. However, despite a southerly aspect, Dove's Nest is definitely to be avoided when wet.

There are some pointers in the 'Getting Started' section at the beginning of the book about climbing in poor conditions. See especially under 'footwear'. However, if you get too wet and cold you won't function properly or have much fun. Having boots that grip on wet rock is not enough if your hands are too numb to grip. In poor conditions a harder but well-protected route may appear preferable to an easier but less safe one. However, while the leader is happily absorbed in the struggle, the poor second frequently gets damp, frozen and thoroughly fed up - sometimes so much so that it becomes virtually impossible to move, let alone climb, when their turn comes. Maybe a scramble, with its potential for continuous movement, is a better bet after all - but with redoubled attention to safety.

Since you're going to get wet anyway, you could go for one of the gill scrambles. If it's the first wet day after a dry spell, the water levels may still be low and the clean, water-washed rock accessible. In sustained wet weather, the serious gill scrambles are best left to the experienced and masochistic. However, easier routes like Sour Milk Gill and Levers Water Beck can be enjoyed in most conditions.

B: Go to a climbing wall

A climbing wall is no substitute for real climbing, but does allow you to stretch muscles and tendons, and to try technically harder climbs in comfort and safety.

There are three walls within easy reach of the Lake District. All have good provision for the lower-grade climber, so just go for the closest.

The *Keswick* wall is in a warehouse behind the Cumberland Pencil Factory, and is well signposted. Head west out of the town centre following signs for Cockermouth, and watch out for a road entrance on the right immediately before the bridge over the river. It has a car park but is easily reached on foot from the town centre – less than five minutes from the bus terminal. It's rather poorly lit, but does offer climbs over a wide range of grades, and is especially popular with school parties. There are plenty of moulded features as well as bolt-on holds, and though the wall is not very high there is lots of scope for variation.

Penrith's wall is based in the leisure centre (with swimming pool and gym as alternative activities). This is at the southern edge of the town. From the large roundabout where A66 crosses M6 (junction 40), take the A66 towards Brough as far as the following roundabout, and there turn left into Penrith. The leisure centre is just left again at the mini roundabout opposite a Shell garage. There is a car park, but once again it's an easy walk from the town centre's bus services, and about 15 minutes (downhill!) from the railway station.

This is a very popular facility, with realistically-graded routes changed regularly by the local climbing club. It's bright and airy and less dusty than most as loose chalk is not allowed. The routes are higher than at Keswick but the floor area is less and the wall can get crowded at times.

The *Kendal* Wall is housed in a large converted factory. It's reached by car off the A6 on the north side of Kendal, and is within walking distance of Kendal railway station.

The main area has some long and impressive climbs (some of them have two whole pitches!) but there are easier routes in smaller chambers at the back, as well as a lot of good bouldering. It's very popular, but extensive enough that queuing for routes is rarely a problem.

C: Go to Trowbarrow

When it's raining in the Lakes it can often be dry only twenty kilometres further south. There are several small natural limestone crags in the area south of Kendal; though rarely above 10m high, they offer pleasant climbing. The most delightful is the Rakes at Hutton Roof (grid ref 567764), with a host of short climbs, many in the easier grades. Because of its size it's easy to arrange a top rope and try something a bit harder than V. Diff. The shortest approach is from near Hutton Roof church, where there is roadside parking. Here and at Trowbarrow, there's a view from the top back to the main Lake District, so you can see if the rain's stopped yet over there!

Trowbarrow (grid ref 481759) is an old limestone quarry, last worked in the 1960s and now a nature reserve. Every time you go, the quarry floor is a little greener. Most of the climbs face west or south, and dry quickly after rain. However, if you get there and it is still raining, beware: the rock is slippery when wet.

The quarry lies about a kilometre east of Silverdale railway station on the Furness Line. From the train, walk east along the road for about five minutes to a sign for Trowbarrow: follow the path into the woods and through the karabiner gate (you'll see) to reach the quarry.

By car, from the A6, follow the signs for Leighton Moss (an important RSPB reserve). There are parking spaces on either side where the road runs into woods, with steps going up to a gap in a fence. Just a few metres into the wood there's a kissing gate, and then the path forks. Take the right branch, which leads in a few minutes to the quarry.

Amenities

There's a tea room at the Leighton Moss RSPB centre, which is pretty handy, especially for those who've arrived by train. A couple of kilometres further west there's an outstanding tea room at Wolf House Gallery. There's a good choice of pubs in the area, of which the nearest as well as one of the best is the New Inn at Yealand Conyers.

68. Original Route 40m V. Diff

Guide time 1/2 hour

The route offers some good climbing and grandstand views of Main Wall. Apparently innocuous, it proves to be quite a serious outing, past and sometimes over some very large blocks which appear to be held in position only by their own weight. Most of the protection relies on these

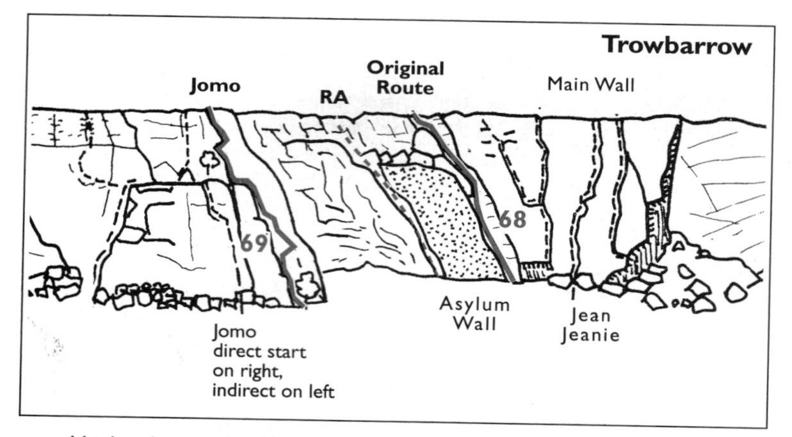

blocks. Approach with caution and be alert for any signs of recent shifts. First climbed in 1967, fairly soon after the cessation of quarrying, and - as the name implies - the first route on the crag.

Approach

The focal point is the near vertical Main Wall. There's nothing here unless you lead at VS, but for anyone who does, the central crackline, Jean Jeanie, is a must. Left of the wall is a more broken and easier angled area of rock called Red Slab. Original Route climbs its left rib.

Start at the base of the rib, below some stacked blocks.

1. (40m) There's a steep start over the blocks, then a delicate slab leads to another block. Just above this is a ledge, with a small elder tree on its right. It is possible to break the pitch here into two virtually equal halves: the best belays are under large blocks just above. But it's better to do the route in one.

Step up just left of the tree. Climb the left edge of the slab above. The slab narrows below a bulge; move round to left of this, then pull up to the right onto a higher band of slab. Move up and again to the right, to finish over large blocks. There are good belays on top of the final block, or you can continue up the short fluted wall behind, to trees.

Trowbarrow with a climber on the Original Route

Descent: follow a narrow path through the trees, parallel to the top of Red Slab, and then round to the right near the top of Main Wall (well worth a look down). Continue in the same direction, above more broken walls, until you meet a solid wooden fence. Step over this and go down an easy slope to the quarry floor.

69. Jomo 36m V. Diff

A fine varied excursion which will test many V. Diff leaders, especially if the direct start is taken. The crucial move is hard enough, and just high enough off the deck, to push the limit of the V. Diff grade. Short people in particular will find it demanding. Like the previous route, climbed in 1967 during the first explorations.

Approach

To the left of Original Route there's a very steep wall with a number of desperate climbs. On this wall's left side is an obvious ramp line, taken by a route called Ramp Ant. (Ramp Ant just rates Severe, with good climbing in the lower two thirds but a more serious and less pleasant finish.)

Climber on the 2nd pitch of Jomo

To left of Ramp Ant's wall is an area of broken rock, but things improve 30m left, where another large buttress projects well out into the quarry floor.

Start: Where the foot of the buttress starts to turn the corner again, you can discern faded yellow paint spelling out 'No Climbing'. Start here.

1. Direct Start (22m) Climb directly through 'No Climbing'. Hah! There's one good handhold at the top of the steepest part, and you can also fiddle in a micro wire here. Once you get your feet to the level of the good hold, things get easier.

(Indirect Start). If this looks too hard, you can climb much easier rock a couple of metres to the left, into an almost-gully. Where the angle of the rock on the right eases, move back onto it across ledges.

By either start, now climb the slab (easy but unprotected) to the base of a prominent diagonal crack. Climb this, with one hard move but good protection, to a large terrace with good block belays.

2. (14m) Climb the left-slanting, stepped corner above the belays to a small ledge below an overhang. Make a tricky move round to right of the overhang using small footholds on the right wall. Finish straight up the fluted wall above.

Descent: The simplest plan is to bushwhack rightwards to the top of Original Route and then follow the descent described from there.

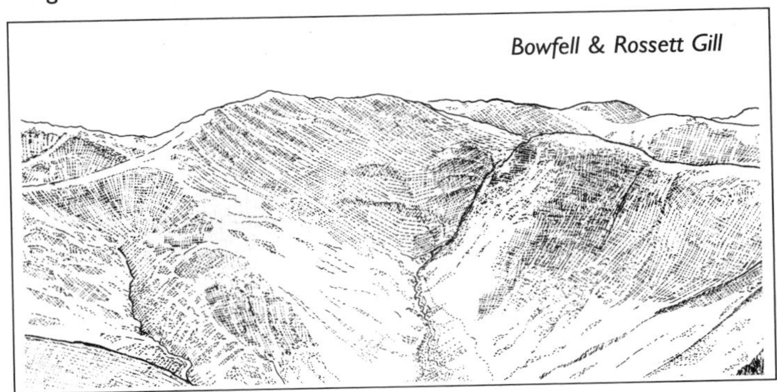
Bowfell & Rossett Gill

Exploring Further

The routes in this book are only the start. There is a wealth of good scrambling and climbing in the Lake District, and it has been extensively recorded. The books listed below are found in outdoor gear shops, especially in the Lakes, but less often in ordinary bookshops. They can also be ordered from their publishers' websites.

Scrambles

The most complete record of scrambles in the district is found in the two volumes by Brian Evans:

Scrambles in the Lake District (revised 1985, ISBN 0 902363 39 5) and *More Scrambles in the Lake District* (published 1990, ISBN 1 85284 042 0) both published by Cicerone Press, 2 Police Square, Milnthorpe, Cumbria LA7 7PY; more information and on-line ordering at www.cicerone.co.uk

These are invaluable books, which will keep even the keenest of scramblers going for a long time. Even so his 160 or so routes don't exhaust the possibilities. It's the nature of scrambling that there are often many ways up a crag, and experienced scramblers will enjoy finding variations and completely new routes such as Troughton Beck. With scrambling routes not being tied to particular lines of handholds, and changing over time due to the passage of scramblers or to rockfall (such as Stepped Ridge, Brown Cove Crags), it's not surprising that our assessment of grades doesn't always tally with those you'd find in Evans. For some routes our grade is lower than his (e.g. Gillercombe NE Buttress) and for others higher (e.g. Pike o' Stickle). Where our routes coincide we find that in the great majority of cases our gradings also coincide: this suggests that scramble grading does have quite a bit of objective reality.

Rock Climbs

Rock climbs follow more precisely defined lines than many scrambles do, so there may be less scope for variation, but even so grading is never an exact science and there are instances where our grades differ from those given in the definitive climbing guides to the District. It all adds to the fun!

The definitive climbing guides to the District are produced by the Fell & Rock Climbing Club. The current 8th series comprises 6 volumes:

Gable and Pillar (1991) by Dave Kirby & Jim Loxham ISBN: 085028 033 8

Buttermere and Eastern Crags (1992) by Rick Graham, Al Davis and Trevor ISBN: 0 85028 036 2

Dow, Duddon and Slate (1994) by Al Phizacklea ISBN: 0 85028 037 0

Scafell, Wasdale and Eskdale (1996) by Al Phizacklea ISBN: 0 85028 038 9

Langdale (1999) by Max Biden ISBN: 0 850028 041 9

Borrowdale (2000) by Gary Baum and Al Hewison ISBN: 0 85028 043 5

These include routes at all grades up to E9. Recent new routes, and changes to existing routes (e.g. from rockfall) can also be tracked through the FRCC's Recent Developments books and on their website, www.frcc.co.uk. Books can be ordered on-line at www.frcc.co.uk/publications/index.htm

There are few new routes being discovered at the Mod - V. Diff grades, though occasional gems do still come to light. So climbers at these grades can manage very well with earlier guidebooks, such as the 6th and 7th Series. However, never forget that routes can change as a result of rockfall or through becoming polished by increasing traffic. A prime example is Napes Needle, originally V. Diff, now graded Hard Severe.

The climbs at Trowbarrow, and elsewhere in the vicinity, are detailed in *Lancashire Rock*, published by the British Mountaineering Council, ISBN 0 903908 17 4.

Learning to climb - or learning to climb better

Anyone wanting to learn more about climbing should contact the British Mountaineering Council (BMC). They can advise on training and put you in touch with climbing clubs in your area. Contact them at 177-179 Burton Road, Manchester M20 2BB; Tel: 0870 010 4878; Fax: 0161 445 4500; email: office@thebmc.co.uk; www.thebmc.co.uk

Many outdoor centres and independent mountain guides run introductory and intermediate courses. There are far too many to list here. You could look in the Yellow Pages under 'Outdoor Pursuits', but be prepared to wade through a lot of paintball and quad bike centres! A better bet is to look in the back of any of the main climbing magazines - *High Mountain Sports, Climber,* and *On the Edge*.

The National Mountain Centre at Plas y Brenin in Snowdonia runs courses specifically for scrambling as well as introductory and more advanced rock climbing. Free brochure on request from Plas y Brenin National Mountain Centre, Capel Curig, Conwy, LL24 OET; Tel: 01690 720214; Fax: 01690 720394; email: info@pyb.co.uk; www.pyb.co.uk

The Scottish equivalent is Glenmore Lodge, Aviemore, Inverness-shire PH22 1QU; Tel: 01479 861256; Fax: 01479 861212; www.glenmorelodge.org.uk

There's no substitute for hands-on experience, but many people have learned to climb safely and well with the help of a good book. A few recommendable titles are:

The Handbook of Climbing, by Alan Fyffe, Iain Peter, Hamish MacInnes (Pelham 1997) ISBN: 0 7207 2054 0

The Beginner's Guide to Rock Climbing, by Malcolm Creasey (Lorenz Books 2000) ISBN: 0 7548 0621 9

The Complete Guide to Rope Techniques, by Nigel Shepherd (Constable Robinson 2002) ISBN: 1 84119 323 2

Waterfalls in the Esk Gorge Photo: Judith Brown

Glossary

Some terms often used in climbing and scrambling

abseil: a method of descending by a (controlled!) slide down a rope. If doubled ropes are used they can be pulled down afterwards. Not to be attempted unless you know exactly what you are doing.

aid: the use of ropes, runners, etc, to help yourself up the climb, rather than just for protection. While the use of aid is a jolly bad show, it is preferable to serious injury or death. However, using aid can sometimes lead you into further difficulties, and it may be better to retreat.

anchor: the actual point of attachment to rock at a belay, or for an abseil.

arete: a sharp rocky ridge, whether horizontal, vertical or in between.

back and foot: a method of climbing a chimney with the back on one wall and the feet on the other.

beck: Lakeland dialect word for a stream.

belay: a multi-purpose word, both noun and verb. It can mean the actual attachment to the rock (the anchor), the act of fixing such an attachment, and the process of managing the rope to protect a partner as they climb. It is also used more loosely to refer to the stance.

bridging: a method of climbing, especially in grooves and corners, with feet spread wide apart on opposing surfaces.

cam, camming device: sophisticated (and expensive) mechanical protection devices. They will fit in parallel-sided and even slightly flared cracks where no ordinary nut is secure. On easier climbs they may be reassuring but are hardly indispensable.

chimney: a fissure in a rock face, wider than a crack but narrower than a gully. More precisely, a chimney is wide enough to get your whole body inside. But if it's too wide to climb by back-and-foot or bridging, it has become a gully.

chockstone: a jammed stone or boulder in a crack, chimney or gully. Can be an aid or an obstacle!

choss, chossy: messy, dirty or loose rock and other debris. Sometimes a general term of disparagement for an undistinguished climb.

crux: the hardest section of a route, usually decisive. Even so, relaxing after the crux is not a good idea!

exposure: in climbing jargon, the presence of a big drop below you. Exposure presents an obvious danger to the unroped, but the roped climber often confronts it in perfect safety - though it can still be scary to those unaccustomed to it.

Friend: a brand (the original, in fact) of camming device, though the term is often used generically.

gangway: a slanting line or upward-sloping ledge on a rock face - usually one that requires climbing rather than walking. May also be called a ramp.

gardening: in climbing terms, not the cultivation of plant life, but its removal from holds and cracks. For obvious environmental reasons, it should be kept to a minimum.

gill: a steep stream, often with cascades and/or ravine sections, which may be suitable for scrambling.

glacis: a very easy-angled area of rock.

hex: a type of nut, usually used in larger sizes. A curse invoked by seconds whose leaders fail to protect traverses.

jam/jamming: a range of methods of wedging fingers, hands, fists, toes, etc in a crack.

jug: (from 'jug-handle'): a large, comforting hand-hold.

karabiner (krab): a spring-loaded clip or snap-link, which the rope can be quickly threaded into.

layaway: a climbing technique of leaning sideways away from a hold to maintain balance.

layback: a technique used to climb a crack in a corner, with feet on the wall and hands on the edge of the crack. It's very strenuous and best done quickly. Alternatives such as jamming or bridging are generally preferable.

leader: in rock-climbing, the first person to climb a pitch.

mantelshelf: a climbing move to gain a ledge on a steep wall, by pushing up to a straight-arm position before bringing a foot onto the ledge.

nut: a piece of metal inserted in a crack for a belay or runner.

peg, piton: a piece of metal with an eye on the end, hammered into a crack. Pegs damage the rock and are rarely used nowadays. Do not carry pegs on any of the routes in this book!

pitch: a section of a climb between belays.

ramp: see gangway.

Rock: a brand of nut, though the term is often used generically.

Rockface: a TV series bearing no resemblance to rock climbing.

runner, running belay: intermediate protection on a pitch. Mostly for the benefit of the leader, but on diagonal and horizontal sections may also be of great benefit to seconds.

second: the second person in a roped team to climb a pitch. Also, in larger teams, the third, fourth, etc.

slab: an area of rock that's basically flat and is neither vertical nor horizontal; usually considered to cover angles between 30 and 75 degrees. Any steeper and it's a wall.

sling:: a closed loop of rope or (more usually) tape, used for belays or runners. Very useful on many easier climbs.

stance: a ledge or other secure place to stop on a rock climb. Normally a place to take a belay at the end of a pitch.

tat: bits of old rope or tape occasionally left on belays or abseil points. May be unsafe and need replacement. Also unsightly and if not necessary should be removed.

thread: a runner or belay formed by threading a sling behind a chockstone or through a natural hole in the rock.

thrutch: an undignified, inelegant and strenuous approach to climbing a crack or chimney. There is normally an alternative!

traverse: a generally horizontal section going across, rather than up, the rockface.

wire: a nut (by one of the above definitions) attached to a short length of wire.

Esk Buttress & Pen

Index of Climbs (Alphabetical)

Index of Climbs

Book Order

Index by Book Order Continued

Index of Climbs

By Grade

Index by Grade Continued

NOTES

NOTES

NOTES

Other Titles from Grey Stone Books

The Famous Highland Drove Walk by Irvine Butterfield
Irvine Butterfield, author of the best-selling High Mountains of Britain and Ireland, takes his readers in the hoofprints of the last cattle drove in 1981, where 29 bullocks and a cow called Matilda recreated a journey across the Highlands of Scotland, from the Isle of Skye to the mart at Crieff in Perthshire. In this 128-page book, he interweaves the story with background history and legend and offers walkers alternative high and low routes, enabling them to plan this romantic journey across seven great mountain ranges, Illustrated with both colour and black and white photos.
Paperback £9.95 ISBN 0951599 6-5-8

Across Scotland on Foot by Ronald Turnbull
Highly acclaimed by the press, this book gives its readers six inspirational coast-to-coast routes across Scotland, plus ideas and practical advice for planning their own. An ideal present for both runners and walkers. 160p 210-148mm
Paperback £5.95 ISBN 0951599 6-4-X

Welsh Three Thousand Foot Challenges by Roy Clayton and Ronald Turnbull
This 128-page book is based around the 27-mile Welsh Threethousands route. While Clayton guides the walkers, Turnbull, an experienced fellrunner, gives the necessary advice for runners and walkers who wish to pick up their pace.. The book includes schedules by record holder Colin Donnelly and former record holder, Joss Naylor as well as detailed advice on diet and injuries. Turnbull also describes in detail the 47-top Paddy Buckley round, which can be done as a one-day run (for the elite) or a 4-day backpack, and the story of near 200-mile Dragon's Back race.
Paperback £5.95 ISBN 0951599 6-6-6

Lakeland Mountain Challenges byRonald Turnbull and Roy Clayton
In the same series as The Welsh Three Thousand Foot Challenges, this book is 160 pages crammed full of information on the Lakeland 3000s, the Old County Tops, the Bob Graham Round, the Roman Road, Penrith to the Sea and the great horseshoe walks.
Paperback£6.95 ISBN 0951599 6-8-2

The Bowland Dales Traverse by John Gillham
The Bowland-Dales Traverse is a long-distance route spanning 85 miles between Garstang near Preston to Richmond in Yorkshire, threading through some of the loveliest hill country of the Forest of Bowland and the Yorkshire Dales. Visited en route are the heather-clad Bowland fells, Slaidburn, Settle, Malham, Kettlewell, Castle Bolton and Reeth. The pocket book is illustrated by line drawings and black & white photo.s 64pages 148X105mm
Paperback £2.95 ISBN 0951599 6-2-3